Arthur ᵥ ᵥillage

The Somerset Childhood of Arthur Westcott
from 1900 - 1915

An autobiography

A fond record of a happy childhood
spent in the Village of Hewish and the
surrounding countryside in Edwardian England
before the changes wrought by the Great War.

We wish to thank all the members of the Congresbury History Group for the help and encouragement they gave to Arthur in the writing and original publication of this book but in particular the following:

Ann Gunner
  - For many hours spent on the word processor
Gill Bedingfield and Chris Short
  - For initial proof reading
Ken Johnson
  - For arranging typesetting & printing

Thanks are also due to the History Group Committee for waiving the copyright in order that the proceeds from the sale of this edition can be donated to the care of abandoned babies in South Africa.

ISBN 0 9510979 5 4

First Published: 1991
Second Impression: 1992
Republished: 2003

Typeset, Designed & Printed By West Country Design
(0800) 389 4766

Front Cover.
Arthur Westcott on the Congresbury railway station platform 1986.
He is wearing his GWR uniform.

Foreword

This edition of Arthurs village is published as a memorial to my father who died in 1997 at the age of 96.

For many years he entertained the family with vivid and humorous accounts of his rural childhood at the start of the 20th century.

He was persuaded to record some of them in his immaculate copperplate script and dedicated the manuscript to his granddaughters. They claim that their knowledge of the social history of the period was much enhanced by his stories.

It was later suggested by members of the Congresbury History Group that they might appeal to a wider public. Thus was born the first edition of this book.

The article at the back of this edition was written by one of those granddaughters who now works as a journalist in Cape Town and is closely concerned with the charity there described.

Arthur loved and was loved by children of all ages and would have been pleased that his little book could raise funds for such a cause.

Patricia Fox

I

ARTHUR JAMES WESTCOTT

My Life   1900 - 1915

To my very dear Grand-daughters

With love

August 1988

HEWISH FROM 1900

To recall one's schooldays in the early years of this century may not seem very sensational until comparisons are made with those of today, and not only schooldays but the way of life of everybody in the village.

Hewish consisted mainly of farm labouring families, consequently living standards were very low, in fact poverty stricken, but this was no means peculiar to our village - the pattern of living in any agricultural community throughout the country would be very similar.

The changes which have occurred during the past sixty years or so are simply astounding - they have altered our way of life more so than any which took place in the previous two or three hundred years and for this reason to recall the conditions under which we lived seem worth recording.

Here is a list of amenities and luxuries unknown to us at that time but which today are commonplace, generally regarded as necessities and taken for granted!

No electricity
No telephones, public or private
No radio, television or fridges
No motor cars or buses
No daily newspaper deliveries in the village
No wellington boots
No Old Age Pensions, National Health Service or Social Security
No unemployment pay
No public water supply or flush lavatories
No bathrooms
No plastic bags or zip fasteners
No drip dry garments
No aluminium kitchen utensils
No stainless steel cutlery
No aeroplanes
No tarred macadam roads
No tinned foods or vacuum flasks

Of course some of the public services were available in the towns, e.g. gas, water and electricity but they were run by small local or municipal undertakings and were not extended into rural areas until they were absorbed in a nationwide network. Electricity was the forerunner of these amenities on account of it being relayed across country by overhead cables.

EARLY DAYS

I was told that I was born on 7 September 1900 and subsequent perusal of my birth certificate confirms this. My entry into the big world was preceded by my twin sister Theresa Gertrude by one hour and ten minutes. We were born at Hewish in the parish of Congresbury where my father was a railway signalman and we lived in the Railway Crossing Cottage. To register our births mother had to walk to Congresbury where the registrar attended periodically at the "Railway Inn" (now the Prince of Wales) and this meant a two and a half mile walk. It was necessary for mother to make the journey as my father's working hours precluded him from carrying out this important legal requirement during the hours when the registrar was in attendance, and of course, it was necessary for mother to take us in the pram. The first great event of our twin existence was our christening at a church in Bridgwater - my mother's home. It was intended that this should have taken place at our church at Hewish, St. Anne's, but owing to my father's hours of duty he could not attend at the Vicar's fixed days for christenings and to perform the service at any other time a fee was payable, so we were taken to Bridgwater and the fee saved went towards a christening party at grandmother's house!

FIRST DAYS AT SCHOOL

We both commenced our schooling at Hewish at the age of 4½ years, in May 1905, but I cannot remember my first days at school. The infant teachers were Mrs Page, the wife of the headmaster, and Miss Frances Page, their daughter. Mr Page taught only in the "big room" and he was nicknamed "Snowball" on account of his mass of white hair and a fine white beard. The infant room had a "gallery" of four or five steps and a row of desks were fixed along each step; my recollections are that we occupied the desks immediately under the window. Mrs Page was very severe and humourless - she rarely smiled and we were afraid of her but Miss Page, who was a cripple using a crutch and wearing a large heavy looking boot on one foot, was very gentle and kind and we were very fond of her.

The Railway Crossing Cottage

We lived about half a mile from the school - the Crossing House was situated on a strip of land between the railway line and a deep rhine (pronounced "rheen" - a Somerset name for an artificial water course for draining the otherwise waterlogged land and taking the water of the neighbouring hills). About three or four miles further down it joined the river Yeo before entering the sea, and at the junction was prevented from becoming tidal by a flood gate.

SCHOOL LESSONS IN THE INFANT ROOM

Our lessons were mainly learning to read and write and as we already knew the alphabet before commencing school through our mother often singing to us in a form of rhyme, we were off to a good start and we soon picked up reading short sentences like "the cat sat on the mat". We used small slates for writing and drawing and our writing lessons were first "pot-hooks" and "hangers" e.g. ƒ ƒ ƒ))) from which we went on to "joining up". We used no exercise books in the infant room and slates were in use throughout the whole school.

I remember how the use of slate pencils made a squeaking noise, and we were supplied with a damp sponge to clean our slates, but they soon wore out - long before our new ones ever arrived, and then we were expected to bring a clean piece of rag from home on Monday mornings - many children of course failed to do so and when teacher's back was turned many of the "failures" spat on their slates and wiped them with their sleeves. I remember too the awful stench of the sponges as they became "stale".

We always commenced each day with a hymn and prayers and this was followed by learning the church Catechism off by heart, through the whole class repeating it over and over again - we also had to learn some hymns by the same method.

Our "sums" in the infant room (we did not use the word arithmetic) consisted mainly of learning our "tables" by similar repetition from "two to twelve" times and how we used to gabble the "ten times" in a sing-song fashion and with increasing speed!

A favourite lesson which did not seem very often was with coloured paper - bright reds, greens and yellows. The "base" consisted of small squares with a row of slits through which we threaded coloured strips in and out to give a basket work effect.

We also learned to do plain knitting - both girls and boys - and the needles were wooden meat skewers, no doubt saved from the schoolmaster's Sunday joints - Mrs Page smoothed them down with sand-paper, and I remember the brown burnt ends, charred too deeply for removal by sandpapering and they had a "roasty" smell! The wool we used was a dirty grey colour and my sisters said it was the selvedge of flannel cloth. Mrs Page gave us our first knitting lesson by having us out one by one to stand by her chair and watch her "cast on" the first row or two of eight or nine stitches - then we went back to our desks to carry on and I hadn't a clue how to proceed, so I wound the wool around the spare needle and spaced it as evenly as possible to look like stitches and then I could go no further. When Mrs Page came round to inspect I had my ears boxed and a scolding to go with it. I went home very worried, probably crying, but my elder sister came to my rescue and showed me how it should be done, which enabled me to do the job properly at the next knitting lesson. After three years in the infants (it may have been two) we were promoted to the big room, commencing in "Standard 1". There were seven or eight scholars seated in long desks and throughout our lessons we moved from first place (top) to seventh or eighth (bottom). The competition to be at the "top" was very keen, the first three or four places were generally held by the brighter lads and we were moved up and down according to how we answered questions. It would be "Westcott move up one" or perhaps two and, of course, downward in the same manner; for bad behaviour we were sent to the bottom - but the brighter ones (which I will say with all due modesty, included me) never worried much when sent to the bottom - we knew we should soon be up in third or fourth place within two or three lessons. The honour of being "top" had the privilege of giving out the slates, pencils or books. This system obtained throughout the school until a new school master arrived in 1910 (Mr J S Gower). On and from Standard 1 we had writing books and used pen and ink. We had "copy books" in which, on each page, the top line was printed in "copperplate" a "proverb" - like "a stitch in time saves nine" - and we had to copy it out on set lines below. But slates, larger ones now, were still used for "sums" in all the Standards.

St Anne's School Hewish. About 1910

THE SCHOOL BELL

School commenced at 9 am and dinner time was from 12 noon to 1.30 pm and one of the early scholars had the honour of ringing the school bell at five minutes to nine and at 1.25 pm. This was no doubt necessary in those days as very few homes had the correct time and probably some were even without clocks. The only way to obtain the correct time was at the railway station (Puxton) or at the signal box. The bell was housed in an elegant little spire with a rope through the ceiling - both spire and bell have since been removed. The pretty spire was four sided with fancy tiles and it seemed to me like some I had seen in a picture of Switzerland.

Many of the children had to walk over two miles from their homes and they were the ones who usually arrived early - some came from Rolstone, Puxton, Heathgate and Wick St Lawrence - and lots of them were from very poor families - mainly farm labourers' children - they were ill-shod, macintoshes and wellington boots were unknown, and many had no overcoats, consequently in wet weather they arrived with soaking wet feet and there were no drying facilities so they had to sit in their wet clothes throughout lessons. Often some stayed at home, through having no good boots, and I remember how the cloakroom stank when full of wet overcoats, and sometimes old hessian sacks. There were no washing facilities, but a few years later a white enamelled bowl and jug were provided on a bare wooden shelf (with a hole in it for the bowl) across one corner of the "lobby" - (it was not known as a cloakroom) - a roller towel and a cake of red carbolic soap were provided with it.

Children arriving late had to stand in the doorway until prayers were said and a hymn sung - for this they were often caned. There was no accommodation for meals and the "dinner children" had to eat their dinners in the playground; for many of the poorer ones this consisted of bread and lard or dripping - none brought any drinks (vacuum flasks too were unknown) and in wet weather they sat at their desks to eat their meals.

WAGES

As a family we were comparatively well off - my father's wage up to the outbreak of the First World War 1914-18 - was twenty two shillings per week for a ten hour day. He and his colleague (Mr Bailey) were no doubt the best paid men in the village. They worked "days and nights" on alternate weeks and as the signal box was open continuously throughout the 24 hours, another man walked from Yatton daily to work the other four in the afternoon. Another signalman came from Yatton on Sunday to enable the change-over from days to nights to be made.

Our house was the best cottage in the village with a large garden. It was railway owned, I believe, and the rent was two shillings and sixpence per week. My father always produced sufficient "taters" and vegetables to keep us all the year round and with a ten hour working day he had to work very hard at gardening as I never knew him to buy vegetables. I think he would have "lost face" if he had to buy a cabbage, and when his potato crop was heavy he even had some to sell! He often kept one or two pigs - one to kill for ourselves and the other to sell. A man came to kill ours in the backyard - all the bacon and ham were salted down and kept for our own consumption but the rest of the pork was immediately sold out to neighbours. Most of them also kept pigs and it seemed a point of honour for neighbours to buy and the compliment was returned whenever they killed their pig. There were of course no fridges and all the surplus meat had to be disposed of immediately. Mother dealt with the chitterlings, and a very messy job it was cleaning them. To clean the "innards", they had to be turned inside out on a long smooth stick. She made white and black puddings and plaited the smaller tubes and I have never tasted any so nice since. With the ears and head she made brawn.

We also kept fowls and hatched our own chickens. Our free range eggs were generally sold to the butcher and the money was always put aside in the "fowls box" to pay for the corn and meal. (All eggs produced everywhere were free range then, as the battery and the deep litter systems had not been introduced). Eggs were always very cheap in the spring time and then and only then did we all have a whole fried egg every morning for breakfast - but as the price went up, we were reduced to half an egg each until they reached a fair market price and then we had an egg only on Sundays. When eggs were at their lowest price, I believe at about 9 pence per dozen (old money) in the spring, it was because nearly everyone kept fowls and the pullets were "coming in to lay", making eggs more plentiful. But within a few weeks prices improved at the rate of one or two pence per dozen weekly. Father specialised in keeping black leghorn fowls. He kept a breeding pen at the bottom of the garden and in the spring sold eggs for hatching. Hatching eggs were sold at thirteen to the dozen (one for luck, I suppose). The fowls' free range was in the field on the other side of the rhine and a thin narrow plank was placed across the bridge which they walked over easily. We children used to walk across it for a "dare" - a tricky effort. It was narrow and bent in the middle with our weight. We never fell off but on a few occasions we fell in by falling off the bank, or when the water was frozen over in the winter and the ice gave way.

WINTER SLIDES AND OTHER WINTER SPORTS

During the winter a spell of hard frosts made the roads very slippery. They were of limestone and not tarmacced in those days. In the wheel marks of the farm carts there were long smooth frozen grooves - delightful slides for we boys and some of the girls. Boys' boots were generally studded with hobnails and were ideal for long slides. (Hobnails were nails with large rounded heads and were used to save wear on the soles). This pastime was frowned on by the grown ups because it was dangerous for horses which were apt to slip and break their legs, but I never knew of this ever happening. We always went out on moonlit nights to indulge in this pastime and on a good long slide boys used to throw water along it to ensure a good frozen surface overnight and of course, when it snowed we had good snowball fights.

Another winter occupation was catching birds with the aid of a round sieve (riddle) which everyone used to sift the ashes when the grate was raked out in the morning, an economical method to save the cinders. The sieve was raised a few inches by placing one edge on a short strip of wood to which was tied a length of string. The boy took the other end and concealed himself and crumbs were scattered under the sieve. When a bird spied the crumbs, it entered and the string was pulled to collapse the sieve - this could only be done during hard weather when the birds were hungry.

SCHOOL GAMES IN THE PLAYGROUND

We had no organised games at school so in the playground we played ring games, boys and girls together. There was a season for marbles, whip tops, skipping ropes and of course, in autumn, there were conkers!

We played marbles in groups of three or four - a ring was scuffed in the dirt and each player "dapped" in one marble to commence play. Then each took a turn by throwing a very large marble called a "toller" and standing at a marked distance, tried to knock out as many marbles as possible, and all marbles knocked outside the ring were claimed by the thrower. After each throw the player had to "dap in" another marble. Very small marbles made of white clay with two or three coloured rings painted around them were obtainable at Marks & Spencer's Penny Bazaar in Bristol (nothing then sold was over a penny!) and they were packed in a cardboard box at, of course, a hundred for a penny. At our post office shop one could buy larger stone-like marbles called "stoners" at only 14 for a penny. The M & S marbles were called "alleys" and such was our sense of values - the alleys were worth two stoners. This was recognised as a rate of exchange and also in play so that when one dapped in an alley one was only dapped in on alternate throws. The bigger boys used to stand around the smaller boys rings when playtime was nearly over and the bell was due to ring to call us back to lessons, then quickly grab as many marbles as possible shouting "scrabbles when the bell rings".

We also played "tally on" along the road on the way to and from school. There were no cars about and we had the whole road to ourselves. For tally on we used the smooth grooves made by a farm cart. A player bowled the marble along it and the other player bowled after it. If he secured a hit he won a marble from his opponent. Incidentally, glass marbles were much in evidence - they were obtained by smashing ginger beer bottles to obtain the glass stopper inside. This type of bottle is now very rare and valuable and no doubt the scarcity is on account of so many being smashed by boys everywhere. The marbles were called "glassers" by the players and the rate of exchange was valued at two for an ordinary marble. The type of bottle I have mentioned is now to be found only in antique shops.

FOOTBALL

We also played football in the playground but never possessed a real football at school until my last couple of years when, in 1913, Mr Farr our schoolmaster, started a football fund. A penny or halfpenny was contributed weekly by many of the scholars until there was sufficient to acquire one. Until then we used an old tennis ball or sometimes a ball of rags tied around with string and our goalposts consisted of a small pile of stones. Mr Farr was keen on football and cricket and often joined us during playtime, and he also organised the only two matches we ever played - one cricket and one football. Our vicar at that time was the Revd Pizey - his previous living was at Mark and he arranged with Mr Farr (who also came to us from Mark school) for a team of Mark boys to visit us for a cricket match. One of their players was a son of Revd Pizey, he came to us in his naval cadet uniform. (He later became Admiral Pizey and now lives in retirement in Somerset). The Mark boys came by train from Highbridge to Puxton and then walked the 2½ miles to Hewish.

Later during the winter a return match was arranged. It had to be football and for this the Hewish team had to walk to Puxton station and then from Highbridge station to Mark. None of us had any real football boots or any other form of football togs. The usual schoolboys' dress then consisted of knickerbockers which buttoned below the knee over stockings. We were given tea in the schoolroom at Mark before the return journey home. We must have walked eight or ten miles. I believe we lost on both occasions!

During those last couple of years at school we also acquired some real cricket equipment - bats and wickets, as a result of the Hewish Cricket Club folding up.

Other games in the playground were; "hares and hounds" from corner to corner, but we could not play "sixty" in the playground as there were no places to hide. We often played this game out of school in friends' orchards. We also played cricket out of school hours until about 1913, in fields adjoining our homes. Our bats were home-made, cut from a plank, and our wickets were willow or ash sticks cut from the hedge. Generally we had only a tennis or rubber ball but some boys possessed a hard cricket ball made of compressed cork. I believe they were bought in Weston super Mare for sixpence!

When I was about 13 years old, I had a whole sixpence to spend. It was August Bank Holiday I believe and I had permission from my mother to cycle into Weston immediately after breakfast to buy a real cricket ball. There was only one bicycle in our family, my mother's - an old Rudge Whitworth fixed wheel and we were very rarely allowed to use it. We all learnt to ride on it before we could reach the pedals but as it was fixed wheel and not free wheel, the pedals conveniently came up for one to catch them for each downward stoke!

FISHING

As the rhine ran alongside our garden the whole length we spent a lot of time fishing. In the spring we caught sticklebacks and loggerheads - this was our name for lazy looking dark brown slippery fish which never swam like sticklebacks but which just wriggled about on the mud and were very easy to catch. Our nets were usually a piece of calico, which mother made into a bag, and then a piece of wire was threaded around the top to keep it open and fastened to a stick. We sometimes caught elvers too but for eels we usually used a fishing rod which consisted of a fairly long stick with a piece of string tied on at one end for a line. A bottle cork made a float to tell when one had a bite, and often a bent pin made a fish hook on which we threaded a small worm for bait.

Sometimes we had real fish hooks - they were threepence a dozen I think and my father kept a few and gave us one occasionally. When we caught an eel or two, my father used to skin them and mother fried them with the bacon for breakfast or sometimes baked them in a dish with vinegar in the oven. When my father cut his hand badly trimming our hedge, he was unable to skin an eel, so we had to do it ourselves - a very slippery slimy operation. One had to cut them right around just below the gills, but not deeply, and then grip the partly severed head to pull the skin down over the tail.

Our summer holidays were always taken early - about mid-June to July (five weeks) and we were back at school during August when other schools took theirs. This was because the school managers were generally farmers and they wanted their sons and other boys to assist in the hay-making.

During summer holidays we rarely met up with other boys for games and until I was about twelve years of age I spent many lonely but nevertheless happy hours fishing along the banks of the rhine, walking up and down watching for eels lying on the mud (presumably basking in the sun). When I spotted one, I gently dropped my hooked worm down in front of its nose - sometimes it snapped at it greedily and I soon landed it on the bank. At other times they darted away quickly as if frightened and took safety in flight. (There were no other coarse fish in our rhine although I remember on one occasion seeing a large "Jack" pike which I followed up and down the rhine in the vain hope of getting it to bite!)

During rainy weather when the water was muddy and when the keechers were cleaning out the rhine, we resorted to clotting or raw balling for eels. For this we had a long pole curved towards the thinner end, to which we attached a ball of worms made by threading several worms from end to end with a needle and thread and gathered up in a loose ball tied directly to the end of the pole. This was held just below the surface of the water. The eels could not be seen of course, but when an eel snapped at the bait, a slight vibration could be felt along the pole. It was then quickly pulled up before the fish could let go, as its teeth were caught in the thread and it could only drop off when the pole was held still on the bank.

Men from the village used this method in season and they usually went out to the river Yeo across the fields, (we always referred to it as the salt water river) and caught large quantities in this manner. The more professional types used a large funnel shaped basket with the stem portion in the water and the exact length of their clotting pole from the little stool on which they sat. The semi-circular basket was flat on one side for pegging in and strongly made of willow. It was probably about two feet wide at the opening - something like this

and the clotting pole was like this

Very large worms were called "yisses" - a local term only. Seeing a man crossing the fields at dusk on his way home always made me think of the ancient Britons with their coracles on their backs, as depicted in our school history books!

Another popular form of eel catching was by means of an eel spear, which was used only by the men. The spear was in the form of three or four flat steel blades, edge to edge, closely spaced, saw-toothed and fixed to a long pole. In use, the men walked along the bank driving the spear in at random and eels lying in the mud at the bottom were caught in this way.

BIRD BAITING

During the winter, another form of sport was bird baiting. On dark nights two men walked along the hedges in the fields, one on each side. The one with a lantern shone it into the hedge, beating the bushes with a stick. His partner stood right opposite with a wide open net and the frightened birds flew straight into it. I believe it was an illegal sport even in those days, but when walking home on a dark evening one could see the light moving along and hear the bushes being beaten in the field. Many small birds must have been caught in an evening and they ended up as a family supper dish!

I remember calling at the house of one of my schoolmates and seeing a huge dish of these birds cooked on the table and judging from the mass of legs sticking upwards, it must have been quite a large number. These occupations were mainly followed by the local labourers with a poaching instinct - there being no other form of game in our area.

1908

In spring after school in the evenings until 6 pm, our tea-time, we often went fishing along the river bank. One of my playmates was Oliver Palmer, and he often fished with me. One evening we were fishing along the rhine, he on one side and I on the other. That evening Oliver caught his very first eel and I saw him running along shouting excitedly; "I've caught an eel! I've caught an eel!" He was grasping the wriggling slippery fish with both hands - he must have left his fishing rod on the bank. It was only the usual stick with a piece of string for a line, so it did not matter much. No boy had a real fishing rod in those days. Oliver lived in Caple's Row at the top of our lane and was from one of the poorer families, (the whole row of four or five cottages were occupied by labourers).

During the summer holidays of that year on 5 July 1908, Oliver died and I lost a playmate - he was eight years old! I remember his mother called to ask my mother if I could "follow" the funeral. My father made a little cross and mother covered it with madonna lilies from her flower garden. I walked with a few other boys of my age (I was also in my eighth year) in procession from the house to the church. It was the custom for the mourners to attend a church service on the Sunday after the funeral, and for this we walked in a similar procession as at the funeral. Generally an appropriate hymn or two was sung.

For Oliver I remember the children's hymn, "There's a friend for little children" was one of them. I never see or smell madonna lilies without thinking of Oliver, even now in my 88th year (1988).

Incidentally, in our churchyard the poorer folks, i.e. those who were not considered respectable, or those who were not church or chapelgoers were always buried on the left hand side of the church drive and on that side there was not a single tombstone, but during quite recent years a few have been erected.

INFANTS - FUNERALS

In those days quite a few babies died in infancy and I remember on one occasion my sister Kathleen with three other girls of similar age acted as bearers for a baby boy from Caple's Row. They led the procession carrying the coffin underhand, slung on white webbing. I remember too on another occasion a father of a baby a few days old, calling at houses to find the vicar who was urgently needed to christen a baby before death intervened. Still-born babies were buried at night by the sexton without ceremony or mourners, and they were buried in one corner of the churchyard - almost a hush-hush affair.

RUNNING AFTER BRAKES

During the summer holidays no boys came fishing with me as the main sport of the poorer boys was running after brakes and wagonettes, of which there were many passing through from Bristol to Weston on day outings. Most of the children ran barefoot and they took up stations in small groups along the road. As a vehicle approached they shouted from one group to the next "a four horse brake" or "wagonette". Then they fell in behind running and shouting "Please sir, chuck me out a copper" and when they dropped out the next group took over. The same procedure was followed in the evening on the return journeys. The day trippers then were often rowdy and some made a call at the local pub, the Full Quart, at the top of our lane. This often resulted in fighting with the locals. We were not allowed to go up and watch this excitement, but we heard all about these drunken orgies from the other children later.

Generally, on each brake was a man playing an accordion or concertina and sometimes a man with his face blackened or an "Aunt

Sally". These entertainers always sat up high beside the driver - I think a brake accommodated 25 to 30 passengers in two rows longways.

THE TWINS - WORSE FOR DRINK

When Gertie, my twin sister, and I were about seven years of age, if on a Saturday the weather was wet, mother kept us in bed until dinner time while she did a lot of cleaning, which included black-leading the kitchen range, which was very hard work. Mother took a pride in making it shine, black-leading the top surface, the oven door and the fender, and polishing the bright steel edges. We were not sorry to be upstairs and out of her way and we played around from room to room, using a bolster pillow as a sledge, pulling each other along the landing.

On one occasion, when in our parents' bedroom, we spied the key in the lock of the big oak blanket cheSt. It was a difficult lock and I believe the key had to be turned twice and held over, but we managed it and tucked away in one corner was a bottle of brandy. Mother kept this as a stand-by for certain illnesses as we were five miles from a doctor, at Banwell. There were of course, no phones and the only way of calling him was by sending someone (a neighbour) in a pony cart or on a bicycle, and there were not many bicycles about. We took out the bottle, each taking a swig and emulating our father when we saw him drinking cider with a neighbour. We raised the bottle with a "Here's health, John". We indulged in several swigs until mother came up to wash Gertie just before dinner time - we boys had to wash downstairs. I must have said or done something to cause mother's displeasure as she boxed my ears as I was about to go downstairs. When I reached the kitchen I was violently sick and I remember thinking "Now mother will be sorry". I went back upstairs and plaintively announced "Mother, I've been sick!" "Put out your tongue and let me smell your breath. You've been drinking the brandy!" I vowed and declared we hadn't. "We couldn't open the box!" Mother dashed to the box and took out the bottle and I remember the startled look on her face when she saw there was less brandy than there should have been. I learned later that she was frightened as she had recently read about a little boy who had died through drinking brandy.

My father was on duty in the signal box and it was the custom for mother to take his dinner out to him. The signal box was nearby, just outside our gate. She used to shout to him and he came down and mother handed him his dinner through the big crossing gates. On this occasion she took me with her and announced to my father that "the twins have been drinking the brandy!" Father had a rolled up newspaper in his hand (their daily paper was sent from Yatton and thrown out of a passing train - father had just picked it up). He looked at me, smacked me lightly across the head with the paper and laughed. "Why the little beggar is drunk" he said and swore, I "reeled". We were in utter disgrace, both sent back to bed and during the rest of the day were often sick, and did not want any dinner.

We were still in disgrace next day (Sunday) and were kept home from morning Sunday school and church. In the evening mother went to church and it was usual for father to meet her afterwards with baby sister Ena in the pram. After mother had left, father sent us out in the lane to wheel Ena up and down while he got ready to meet her and we were to accompany him. Whilst in charge of the pram we quarrelled and this resulted in the pram being tipped upside down with the screaming baby underneath. Mr Bailey, father's opposite number, was on duty in the signal box - he rushed down and put the pram the right way up. Now we were in utter disgrace again! Back to bed we had to go and stay there while father went to meet mother, Harold and Kathleen. When mother was informed of our further disgrace I think her heart melted and she thought the twins had had enough. She sent Harold home to tell us we could get up and go to join them, but Gertie sulked and decided to stay in bed!

Perambulators were then quite different from present day patterns and ours had two large wheels about the size of bicycle wheels and with two much smaller leading wheels and a pair of high curved handles. It was bought for Harold, the oldest of us and then was handed down for each new arrival. Fortunately, it was made to accommodate two passengers so that when we twins arrived, it did not necessitate an extra expense to acquire another vehicle.

It was used for all of us long after it was generally considered necessary as mother often went to Bridgwater to visit her parents and it was two and a half miles to Puxton railway station. There was a well in the centre of the pram with a cover for use when the baby was in the lying down position. It could also be opened or folded back to form a second seat and then two could sit up with their legs in the well. I can remember riding in it on these occasions, with little Harold and Kathleen running alongside holding onto mother's skirts. Mother must have risen very early to get us all dressed for these visits - usually they were only day visits - and after walking back from Puxton at night, mother must have found it a very tiring day. She could not rest until we were all undressed and tucked up in bed. I now realise what a hard life it must have been for mother right through our childhood, when I recall the lack of amenities, which are now commonplace in every home no matter how isolated.

DRINKING WATER FROM THE RHINE

All water for cooking and drinking purposes had to be dipped by bucket from the rhine near our back door. It was considered unfit for drinking as it was polluted by drainage from farmyards, etc. and we children were forbidden to drink it until it had been filtered. Our railway cottage was fitted with a special filter. All the children of the village drank it raw and when at play near the water would cup their hands and quench their thirst directly. There was a dipping place outside the lane with steps and a handrail, presumably provided by the local council, and this was used by all the families at our end of the village.

When fathers finished work it was their first duty to fetch water and for this most of them had a yoke for carrying two buckets full with a minimum of spilling. The yoke consisted of a wooden unit shaped to rest comfortably on the shoulders, with a cut-out to fit around the neck and a chain hung at each end to carry a bucket. They were in general use then on the farms for carrying the milk pails from milking shed to dairy, but the article is now considered antique and are to be found only in museums. Often of course, the bigger boys of a family had to do the water fetching after school to save fathers the duty, as the working day did not finish until 6 pm.

Another ingenious method of carrying two buckets of water was by means of a wooden square like a large picture frame. The carrier stood inside the frame resting it on the top of the buckets with the handles on the outside, then as he walked he pulled the handles towards him, and the buckets could be carried steadily without slopping the contents, and the buckets were well away from the carrier's legs.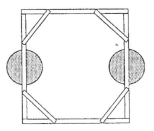

WATER

There were no fresh water springs at Hewish. The farms and some of the cottages had a well dug near the house but they contained only surface water and it was far from pure. Some were connected by a pump fixed in the scullery.

In very hot weather the schoolmaster sent two of the bigger boys down to the bow just below the school to fetch a bucket of water from the river for the children to drink during playtime. (the bucket was the heavy galvanised iron article used by the school cleaner when scrubbing the floors). It was placed in the corner of the playground and an enamelled mug was provided for the use of any thirsty child. This water was equally impure as that of the rhine.

Our vicar, the Revd C R Blathwayt, being wealthy, paid Mr Light at the shop to fetch, twice weekly, two large seventeen gallon milk churns by horse and cart from a spring in somebody's garden at Congresbury.

We had two large water butts outside our back door to catch the rainwater off the roof - this was used for the weekly wash, when mother had to fill the copper boiler and keep the fire going underneath. In our house it was a regular Monday performance and when the washing was done and hung out on the clothes line in the garden, the copper had to be dipped out with a dipping bowl.

The rain water was also used for our bath night - usually Fridays, when we had our weekly bath in the kitchen for which mother kept an extra large zinc bath tub - and what a performance that was! Here again the water had to be dipped out, or carried out, and during the baths the temperature had to be maintained by adding a kettle of boiling water occasionally. If the kettle took a long time to boil the last one or two had to endure the misery of tepid water.

We had a kitchen range and a large kettle of water, about six pints, was always kept simmering and from which a small kettle was filled to bring to the boil quickly for making tea at breakfast and tea time. In winter, the girls had warm water to wash in before school, and they always washed upstairs in their bedroom where they had a washstand with a large china bowl and jug. The heavy demand for hot water for the girls and for our breakfast tea precluded we boys from having the luxury of warm water for our ablutions. These were taken in a handbowl on a bench in the scullery with cold water and on very cold mornings we had to break the ice on the rain water butt! We were quite pleased to boast that we had washed in cold water with lumps of ice floating in it. It was quite obvious that many boys at school did not wash at all on cold mornings and who could blame them? They had to brave the sarcastic remarks of the headmaster who pointed out the dirty water mark around their necks above their coat collars!

Brother Harold and I had to polish our own and our sisters' boots each morning and in those days we were unacquainted with tins of boot polish like Cherry Blossom. At 1d per tin it was considered too expensive. In later years though we used it on our Sunday best footwear. Our Sunday boots were always lighter than our weekday ones and of a softer leather which polished to a good shine more easily than did the blacking on the heavier and stiffer leather of our workday boots. The blacking for these came in cubes, like slabs of chocolate, wrapped in a green greaseproof paper marked Berrys or Day Martin. I think and I believe they were three pence per dozen slabs. The cakes were a black oily mess. We usually cut a slab in half and mashed it up in a little water in the cover of a tin - it required a lot of elbow grease to produce a shine. When the boots were damp it was impossible although when a shine was produced it lasted for most of the day and was waterproof. Incidentally, the cakes and blacking always made me think of mackerel as the name on the wrapping and the blacking showing through the greaseproof was not unlike the markings of that delectable fish.

FATHER - BOOT REPAIRS AND VISITS TO BRISTOL

Our lightweight Sunday boots were worn weekdays during the Summer - otherwise we would have grown out of them before they were worn out. How good it felt to wear such lighter footwear - we could run so much faster! My father always did our boot repairs, soling and heeling, stitching and hobnailing. For the stitching he used waxed thread with a waxed end into which was fitted a pig's bristle in place of a needle. It was the professional method and I believe he learnt it by observing a shoemaker. It was obviously easier to pull in and out of the stitching holes made in the leather with an awl. The use of an ordinary needle with doubled thread would be more difficult to pull in and out. The bristles were bought in small bundles of about a dozen at the shop where father bought his leather, in Redcliffe Street, Bristol. He usually went up in the morning after coming off nights, walking the line to Yatton to catch his train and returning about midday. During the early years of the century I heard father say that a dentist from Weston had a surgery in Clevedon, and when waiting at Yatton for the Clevedon train, he would pull out railwaymen's teeth in the waiting room, either free of charge or at a reduced fee. I am not sure which!

When father arrived home from Bristol on these occasions it was noticed that he produced a box or two of Swan Vestas matches. They were 1d per box and as ordinary matches were about 3d a dozen, it was a real extravagance. He also produced a few pairs of bootlaces and it was not until I was old enough to accompany him, if it was on a Saturday as a special treat, that I discovered the reason for these purchases.

In those days, on most busy streets, there would be a blind or severely crippled man or woman, offering matches or shoe laces for sale and when I went with him father would give me the penny and tell me to go to the person and make the purchase.

POOR BRISTOL CHILDREN
- BLIND BEGGARS AT BRISTOL

This was, I think, father's way of providing a practical example of remembering that there were many unfortunate folk around who were not so well off as ourselves and I hope the lesson was not lost upon me. I remember on one occasion, when I accompanied him to Bristol, it was a very cold wet miserable day and there were many ill clad urchins, boys and girls, running the streets and when father and I went into a shop to buy some bananas, (he often brought a few home as a treat for us children) some of these urchins followed us to the doorway, begging for either money or food. This must have impressed me sufficiently to talk about it when we arrived home because I remembered mother remarking "Those poor children, I think when they are driven to beg like that they must be starving". I remember in particular too that at the base of the railings on Bristol bridge, at one end there was a blind man sitting on a sack holding out a tin mug. I think that same man sat on the same spot in all weathers for quite a few years, for I remember seeing him there after I left school in 1915.

There were always groups of children poorly clad roaming the streets barefoot, especially during school holidays. I recall watching a group in Magpie Park on the centre in more recent years - probably just prior to the introduction of the Welfare State. Vera and I were waiting to catch a bus one summer evening. The group consisted of boys and girls, ages about 9-11 years. Among them was a chubby lad with a peg-leg, his leg apparently amputated at the knee. They were playing around when peg-leg spied a chunk of cake which someone less hungry had apparently tossed into the bushes. (Magpie Park then had a large island shrubbery of rough looking bushes and was fenced around with a strand or two of wire no higher than about 1' 18") While peg-leg was happily munching his cake, one mischievous looking girl conspired with the others to sit on the wire altogether between a pair of posts. The wire was very slack hut as they sat together, their weight took up the slack, and when peg-leg decided to sit he had to do so between the next posts where the wire was taut. Then, at a given signal the group jumped up suddenly, causing peg-leg's section to drop equally suddenly, tipping him, cake and all, into the shrubbery with his legs in the air. They all thought it a great joke and peg-leg was not at all abashed but came up smiling, recovered his cake, and went on munching happily! The shrubbery is now cleared away and no longer do we see little crowds of ragged urchins wandering around aimlessly looking for mischief.

BOOT BLACKS

Another common sight in a busy city street was a boot black. They occupied strategic sites on the kerb at street corners and their clients were mainly city gents going to and fro between their offices and the railway station. Their stand consisted of a wooden block, surmounted by another in the shape of a foot, with the tools of the trade, brushes and polish, lying beside it. I have seen a gentleman nonchalantly reading his newspaper with his foot on the block, and the shoe black on his knees vigorously polishing his boot with brushes and pads. On the sides of the block were generally displayed enamelled plates advertising some well-known boot polish.

There was a bootblack who had a regular stand on Temple Meads Station where he was able to operate in all weathers. Now with cleaner streets, since the disappearance of horse traffic, one's shoes can remain clean all day, resulting in there being no call for the trade of the shoeblacks. City men then often wore buttonup boots in place of laces, generally with 8 or 9 buttons, necessitating the use of a button hook, and always black boots - never brown! Now that little implement is rarely seen but in those days one was generally included in a set of men's hair and clothes brushes. It was only in later years that shoes for men became popular and for the same reason, ie cleaner streets.

EARLY SCHOOL DAYS

During my school days, when in the infants, I generally sat next to Oliver Beacham, a lad about my own age. He was one of a large family of the farm labouring class. Consequently, they were very poor and he was generally clad in someone's left-off clothing, obviously ill fitting - but Oliver was a bright lad and was very good at his lessons. Right through his school days he proved a very good scholar, but owing to poverty there was no outlet for him to take a post where be could use his scholarly attainments for advancement. Consequently, he went farm labouring until in later years he, with others, emigrated to British Columbia where he made good and spent the rest of his life. He became a prominent church worker and was one of the founders when a new church was built. His son also entered the church and became ordained. I never saw Oliver after leaving school in 1915, until in recent years when he came to England on holiday and I learned his history.

But returning to our early school days. It was about 1907 when in the infants, Oliver's eldest sister who had left school, and was about 15 or 16 years of age, was found killed on the railway line at a local level crossing. This of course, was sensational. It proved to be suicide and it was said her father turned her out for reasons which were never revealed to us, but he had the reputation of being a hard parent. His children were never allowed to take part in any school activities or attend any school treats or outings. Poor Oliver! I got on very well with him at school but as he lived over 2 miles away in the Rolstone area, we never met after school or during the holidays. He was such a good tempered and easy going lad and I have vivid memories in later years of him with a broad smile on the way to school during autumn mornings, munching a very big apple and with a coat much too big for him, with large poacher pockets bulging with apples and there was always one for me as soon as we met. I remember during our last days at school, Oliver talking wistfully to me knowing I was going to start a career on the railway. "Of course" he said, "your family is "respectable" and mine isn't!" What a horrible word that was when used in that context. The term 'not respectable' was used to denote the families who were poor and did not mix and went neither to church or chapel. Looking back I think I felt horribly smug when Oliver said it, but now I should feel very ashamed.

CHURCH & CHAPEL - SOCIAL & WEEKDAY EVENTS

During the winter months we attended children's Band of Hope meetings one evening a fortnight and Christian Endeavour one evening weekly. These were chapel events, and we were allowed to be members as there was nothing for children organised by the church. The Christian Endeavour for juniors was a devotional service where a child was selected to read a short story from The Christian Herald, and to give out the hymns. The Band of Hope was a temperance organisation and the theme was always on total abstinence at a time when drinking and drunkenness were rife in every village. We always enjoyed the Band of Hope as we were allowed to recite poems or read a story, generally relating to the cause of total abstinence. We sang rollicking Band of Hope songs and won prizes for good attendance. The chapel folk seemed always more friendly than church folk and they maintained a friendly contact with neighbouring chapels at Milton or Worle.

During the winter months, their members visited our Palmer's Elm Chapel and entertained us with plays and sketches. The chapel also arranged occasional visits of Service of Song, which we all enjoyed as one member read an interesting story and the accompanying choir rendered lively choruses at intervals, having a bearing on the story. We all enjoyed these meetings and also the teas arranged on certain occasions. At that period the church and chapel maintained a very marked aloofness. During one winter, the church did organise a childrens' Band of Hope but it lacked the liveliness of the chapel meetings. It was conducted by the vicar's wife and we asked riddles, did knitting and sang one or two choruses. I recall one or two of the rougher type boys even asking some very rude riddles and on one occasion I with two or three other boys were turned out for bad behaviour. I remember that running out of school we encountered our headmaster, Mr Page, who was strolling down the playground smoking his pipe, as was a habit of his. It was of course very dark but he recognised our voices. When we were out on the road, we waited for the others. It was essential for me to entreat my sisters to refrain from telling my parents and they realising the serious view which would be taken, agreed! But the next morning at school Mr Page raised the subject and wanted to know more about it. In my case, he asked if my parents were told and when the answer was a very meek "No sir", he said "Well, I shall make a point of telling them when I see them". So for several days I went in fear of him telling my parents but fortunately he never did! That Band of Hope lasted only one winter, to no-one's regret - it was generally regarded as a "flop!"

VANDALISM

While various minor offences by schoolboys were committed, there were no occasions of vandalism on the scale existing everywhere today. The one outstanding occurrence I recall was on a Sunday morning, during the Christmas holidays, when we were all assembled in the school playground awaiting the arrival of the Sunday school teacher to open the school. One lad picked up a stone and smashed a window - this was the signal for one or two others to do the same and within a few minutes nearly every window was smashed by the time Miss Champion, the Sunday school teacher, arrived. Knowing what would be in store for me when my parents were told I prudently refrained from taking part in this orgy of destruction. I remember hearing the offenders had to appear at the vicarage to receive a good dressing down from the Rev C R Blathwayt. Only in very recent years was I informed by the ring leader, Arthur Kimmins, that he was made to say a prayer and receive a thrashing!

DUCKING IN THE RHINE

During the years about 1909-10 I had two serious duckings and on one occasion brother Harold came to the rescue and saved me from drowning. It was after a spell of very heavy rains and the ditches were full almost to the level of the banks. We were on the way home from school and just before parting from one of my school mates, we were playing touch and we ended up on a very narrow bridge with a handrail. In my endeavour to make him the last man touch I fell off the bridge and found myself in very deep water. My friend did not realise the serious condition I was in and ran away laughing! Fortunately Harold was nearby and saw me disappear and I remember coming to the surface sufficiently to see through a thin film of water and then down I sank again. The next time I came nearly to the surface there was Harold lying on his tummy across the narrow plank of the bridge and groping for me, and he pulled me out, but I had a very narrow escape. When I went indoors with water dripping from my clothes mother did not realise the serious position and my narrow escape, she was therefore very cross as I was wearing heavy corduroy trousers and she was more concerned about the problem of drying them!

Here I may add that after leaving school, when I was about 16 years old, Harold again saved me from drowning in the river. It was while we were both on the railway at Wookey and came home together for the weekend. On the Sunday morning, we went across the fields to bathe in the river. Harold was a strong swimmer but I was only a learner, so while he swam up and down I was content to swim across from side to side, but when halfway across I dropped and could not recover. Again I remember coming sufficiently to the surface to see the sky through a film of brownish water. There were some boys on a bridge watching us and when they saw only my head above the water they shouted to Harold, and he swam to my rescue. It was an experience for him, as he told me how I struggled and grabbed hold of him with the risk of us both drowning. The field was low lying, and the water was level with the bank and he managed to throw me out and I found myself lying on the warm grass with the water pouring out of me! I was none the worse for the experience but such was the effect on Harold, he never entered the water for a swim throughout the rest of his life!

I had another nasty ducking during the winter of 1909 or 10 after a spell of deep snow. The thaw had set in and the snow had gone from the roads. The fields were still covered and with a playmate we decided to cross the bridge over the ditch and fill our trucks. So with a load of snow, we put the trucks astride the bridge and commenced a push and pull method. I did the pulling between the shafts or handles and the truck overbalanced and I with it. This meant another soaking and again poor mother had a heavy pair of corduroys to dry. Fortunately on this occasion I was able to pull myself out!

A STOLEN DINNER

Compared with present day standards, that of honesty stood very high in school, but one incident at school stands out very clearly in my mind. It involved a girl who stole another girl's dinner from her bag hung up in the lobby (cloakroom). She was, of course, soon discovered and when afternoon lessons were about to commence the offender had to stand before the whole class to receive a lecture. Then she was made to stand still up in the high window for the rest of the afternoon facing the whole school, holding a slate on which was printed in large letters "I AM A THIEF!" This of course made a great impression on us all and the seriousness of the crime was certainly brought home to us. I now question the harsh punishment meted out to this poor girl who most certainly must have been very hungry. It probably left her with a bitter memory throughout her life!

EXERCISES OF SCHOOL DISCIPLINE AFTER HOURS

While walking in the village one evening, Mr J S Gowar encountered one of his scholars smoking a cigarette. The boy was in the company of a young man and the next morning, when he arrived at school, Mr Gowar called him out before the class and spoke to him very severely prior to administering the cane. Probably reminding him that being under age he was breaking the law! Much amusement was caused in the class (even the headmaster could not conceal a smile) when the lad in an effort of self-defence tearfully offered the excuse that "He only gid (gave) I a whiff sir!"

It is questionable whether such discipline could be exercised today for an offence committed off the school premises and after school hours.

I cannot recall ever receiving a caning throughout my school career but I am fairly certain I must have suffered a few strokes when in the lower standards, appropriate to various minor misdemeanours. When in the higher standards at age 12 or 13 I was condemned on several occasions to stay in after school for talking in class and the punishment was to write one hundred lines on "I must not talk in class". On one occasion (probably the last) I had to memorise the first twenty lines of "The quarrel between Brutus and Cassius" from "Julius Caesar". In an endeavour to memorise them, (I hadn't the slightest idea what it was all about!) I commenced to memorise the first two lines and when I came to the second line "You have condemned and noted Lucius Pella" - who, or what was a "Lucius Pella?" I did not get very far with the memorising and eventually the school master gave up and let me leave. I think I was keeping him from his tea! The detention was punishment enough! I eventually learnt the lines with the rest of the class during lessons and then later when I understood them, they were a source of pleasure.

SCHOOL EXAMINATIONS

When Mr Farr came in place of Mr Gowar in 1912 he introduced a monthly system of examinations in the higher standards. He duplicated the results for the information of the parents, in the form of a report. In it were shown the marks awarded for each subject and the position of each pupil in the class. My father followed these reports with keen intereSt. It displeased him to see I was generally third or fourth down the list and it became a sore point with him to see that our neighbour's son, Frank Williams, was always a few marks above me. Frank was about my age, so father used him as a criterion when he read the results. Month after month I took the reports to father and received a wigging on each occasion. How I dreaded those reports!

Then father tried a new tactic. "Look here my son, when you bring a report showing you above Frank, you shall have a watch and chain!" At last it happened! I joyfully carried home a report showing me above Frank and I became the proud possessor of a watch! Now a watch was something to be prized, as only two boys in the school had one and I was particularly pleased as I could carry Greenwich time to Mr Farr each morning as I obtained it from the signal box. That was the only way Greenwich time was recorded in those days, as it came through each morning at 10 o'clock by telephone. Fortunately for me, Frank left school to go to Sexey's school at Blackford, so no further comparisons could be made.

JUMPING DITCHES AND HEDGES

When on the way home from school or when wandering around the fields birdnesting, or during the blackberry season, we often jumped ditches. It was always a contest and it often ended with one boy failing to clear the ditch and landing on the edge in the water, resulting in wet feet and sometimes boots covered with stinking black mud.

During one season of hedge jumping, the bigger boys started jumping through a hedge bordering one of Farmer Champion's fields resulting in making large gaps where sheep or cattle could get through and stray onto the road. One lad, Bert Neath, was seen doing it by Farmer Champion and he summoned him, resulting in his parents being fined half a crown (12½ p). This caused an uproar as Bert's family were chapel members and they were not slow in saying Farmer Champion waited to catch him in preference to any church going lads (of which, no doubt, my brother Harold was one). Farmer Champion was churchwarden and a school manager. I am inclined to think it was righteous wrath on the part of the Neath family!

BLIND MAN'S BUFF - A VARIATION

During the Easter holiday in 1911 or 12, I with three boys of my age, wandered around the fields birdnesting and down our lane from the crossing was an orchard where in due season we did our scrumping for apples. The tenant lived about four miles away so we were free to roam around without risk of discovery. In one corner of the orchard was a cattle shed and feeding stalls and in looking around inside for birds nests we discovered a hen's nest containing three or four eggs. These belonged to a farmer whose house and farmyard were about two hundred yards further down the lane and their poultry had a free range. It was understood that whenever we found a hen laying out on informing Mrs W the farmer's wife, a reward of one penny was forthcoming, so we took the eggs down to Mrs W telling her where we found the neSt. "Oh!" said Mrs W. "That was very good of you but Mr W discovered that nest early this morning and he left the eggs to ensure the hen continued laying there and eventually hatching a brood of chicks, so would you mind taking them back?" Of course this meant no penny came our way! We took them back but in the orchard we placed one egg at a time in the grass, each boy was blindfolded in turn, and after turning him round two or three times he, then armed with a stick, walked two or three paces in what he thought was the direction where the egg lay, and then tried to smash it. We all took turns until all the eggs were smashed and then went on our way rejoicing! This I think was the nearest approach to an act of vandalism in which I ever indulged!

FIGHTS AMONG SCHOOL BOYS

I think fighting among school boys was more common than nowadays. Petty quarrels often ended in a scrap on the way home from school and even some of the girls of the rougher type were not unknown to indulge in hair pulling and face scratching! A fight was, of course, good entertainment for the onlookers who gathered around in a ring and made comments on the merits and demerits of the combatants. Eventually one of them had enough and gave in and afterwards no ill feelings were engendered.

I recall one amusing incident when brother Harold boxed Susan Champion's ears. It happened thus. Susan, with one or two more arrived late for school, after the bell had stopped and the school assembled for prayers. Now latecomers had to stand in the porch where through the open door they could see the class engaged in the opening prayers. After which they came in and stood together to offer explanations of late arrival and to receive punishments. Generally it meant staying in after lessons. Now Susan was a daughter of one of the school managers and it was generally acknowledged that in consequence she did not usually qualify for any punishments so readily as other pupils. On this particular occasion, with a view to averting any forthcoming reprimand, she straightway offered "Please sir, Harold Westcott had his eyes open during prayers and was laughing at us in the doorway". This was a ploy to divert any punishment forthcoming to Harold and the schoolmaster found it a good excuse to vent his anger towards him instead of Susan. So, on the way home, Harold boxed Susan's ears which sent her home crying.

Now it so happened that on Monday mornings Mr Champion, with a grown up son, was to be seen driving to market in a high pony trap, and on our way to school they were often driving across their long drive towards the big gate, leading on to the road. When a boy saw them converging on the gate, there was a rush to open and close it afterwards. This of course saved the laborious effort of the rider climbing down to do it himself and usually a penny was thrown out with a smiling "thank you!". Now, on the Monday following Harold's treatment of Susan, as we were on the way to school, and seeing Farmer Champion driving towards the gate, we raced to reach it first, but Harold being 3 years older than I, outran me and opened the gate. Farmer Champion drove through and stopped with a "Now shut the gate Harold!" and then "Now look here Harold, the next time you hit our Susie, I'll horsewhip you!" Poor Harold dropped back looking rather sheepish and pennyless. In our day, Harold's treatment of Susan would not have been described as boxing her ears but in common parlance and less refined, "He clouted her one under the 'yer-ole!'"

I was once involved in a fight with Durby Davis and for what could be said in a very honourable cause. One morning during lessons, Durby sat at a desk immediately behind my sister Gertie, and he began dipping the ends of her very long hair in the inkwell! Here was a just cause for teaching Durby a lesson, so during the dinner hour we fought long and hard but the issue was not decided, so we resumed after school in the afternoon. In the end I had to give in and acknowledge Durby as the victor but we soon resumed our friendship and I for my part, though beaten, felt that honour was satisfied.

WEAKLING AND BEING "BREECHED"

Until I was about six years of age, I was a very delicate little chap and had to stay home from school during the winter. I had a bed on the floor in the corner of the kitchen which was very warm from the kitchen stove. Gertie often stayed home to keep me company. At that time my father kept a separate pen of fancy poultry - Silver Spangled Hamburgs - and I then regarded them as mine as I had eggs from them to build me up. In cold weather I had no energy to run about and play but used to stand about and shiver. I remember on such an occasion I was up at a neighbours with other children and the kindly woman of the house saw how miserable I looked. "Oh you poor little chap" she said, gave me a kiss and sent me home. But thanks to my mother's tender nursing, I recovered and was able to play and hold my own with other boys of my age. It is quite probable that had I been one in the family of the poorer folk, I would not have survived. Now here I am, hale and hearty, without an ache or pain in my 88th year!

When I was between three or four years I was breeched, ie put into trousers. No boys from that age ever wore skirts and it was quite an occasion. My mother made my first pair from an old suit of father's. I remember wearing them for the first time. Mother carrying me out to show father who was working in the garden. Gertie was upset at the time because she could not be breeched, but then it was unthinkable for any girl to wear anything other than skirts!

Arthur & Gertrude Westcott
at Hewish Crossing c.1903

SUNDAY SCHOOL

We all had to attend Sunday School at 10 am in the morning and 3 pm in the afternoon. We had to attend as soon as we commenced weekday school. After the morning attendance we had to go straight into church for the morning service at 11 am and as my parents were regular churchgoers we usually attended the 6.30 pm evening service as well. Mr Page, the headmaster always conducted the morning school but I believe his daughter, Miss Page (the cripple) took the afternoon school, when she read a story. As we grew older we had to learn the Collect appointed for the day (vide the Church of England Prayer Book) in time to repeat it when we arrived.

After Mr Page left on retirement in 1910, our teachers at Sunday School were the Misses Champion, Farmer Champion's daughters. Sunday scholars were rewarded with three treats annually - a tea party in the school room on Whit Sunday, one at Christmas when prizes were awarded and an outing to Weston super Mare during the summer. We had to take our own mugs for the teas at Whitsun and Christmas. At Whitsun we played games after tea in the paddock behind the church and the highlight of the evening was the scrabble for sweets. The vicar's wife, Mrs Robinson, sat in a chair (she reminded me of Queen Victoria in a large black dress, reaching to her ankles) with a large jar of sweets, usually those pear shaped acid drop kind - red on one side and yellow on the other. She scattered them in the long grass and then we "scrabbled" for them, picking up as many as possible with plenty of grass stuck to them, which was a mere detail!

Our summer outing to Weston super Mare was in the hay wagons of Farmers Champion and FroSt. Boards were placed across and we sat in rows. We spent the day on the beach and with generally two pence to spend, which was usually allocated to a penny donkey ride and two half penny cornets of ice cream. Ice cream in those days was only obtainable on the beach, never in shops or restaurants - this being the days before refrigerators. The ice cream man, usually an Italian, had an ice cream cart, a two-wheeled barrow with a coloured canvas canopy. The ice cream was in a deep canister packed around with ice, and the ice cream man wore a white sleeve on one arm as a mark of cleanliness when dipping down into the canister. So you can imagine the ice cream was a real treat for us!

We all assembled at a restaurant for tea and then went to a cobbled stone stable yard to climb into the wagons homeward bound. I remember how the heavy carthorses almost galloped home and the driver, one of the farmer's grown up sons, had difficulty in holding them back! I can never remember a wet day on those outings - fortunately for us, as we had no covering over the wagons. The chapel Sunday School had similar outings but not on the same days. For the church Sunday School, the weekday school was closed but the chapel children had to absent themselves.

Here I may recall an amusing incident relating to myself. I was about seven years of age, when on the Sunday School outing after tea I had to appeal to mother as I was in great distress in urgent need of the toilet. Mother gave me a penny and told Harold to take me to the public lavatories. At that time they were in charge of an attendant who took your money and then unlocked a door for you to enter. According to Harold, I rushed up to the attendant shouting "a pennyworth please!" How Harold teased me about that incident and often joked about it over the years!

Our Sunday School Christmas treat was a tea in the school room during the holidays when prizes for regular attendance were awarded. Coronation mugs were much in evidence then and mother always tied some coloured wool on ours to prevent any sly swapping for another child's which was probably badly chipped! The evening was then taken up with party games like Blind Man's Buff or Spinning the Trencher, etc.

THE REVEREND HAINES - VICAR OF PUXTON

About 1909 our vicar, the Revd T A Robinson died, and we had visiting priests during the interregnum and often one came from Weston - the Revd Haines. It was said he was without a living and on his earlier visits he used to walk the six miles to conduct our services but when he became a regular visitor the churchwardens fetched him by pony and trap and entertained him for lunch. It was said that he was "down and out" and could not secure a living. On this account, as the Hewish St Anne's living also took in St Saviour's at Puxton, it was decided to break it up and when a new incumbent was appointed, the Revd Haines was awarded the Puxton living.

The Revd T A Robinson's successor was the Revd Pizey from Mark and unfortunately the very few Puxton folks who were churchgoing had for years attached themselves to St Anne's Hewish and one of them had become churchwarden at Hewish. None of them supported the new incumbent at Puxton. Consequently, a regular

Sunday service was there for several years conducted without a single member in the congregation! He had no churchwarden and no organist but the vicar faithfully observed the prescribed prayer book service Sunday by Sunday. This sorry condition was confirmed by Hewish residents who occasionally visited the church out of curiosity! There was of course no vicarage at Puxton and during his incumbency the Revd Haines resided in Clevedon, and cycled to and fro. Several years later when at home for the weekend, I, with a friend Frank Smith, visited the church when out for a Sunday morning walk and arrived just as he was concluding the service. He was very pleased to show us around and opened the old chest and produced many of the old documents. He was obviously fully conversant with their contents, giving us a very interesting commentary. He then directed us to the tower and he followed us up. At the top was a small square opening to get out onto the roof. As the vicar followed us in getting through the opening, he became jammed. When one pushed a leg through there was a drop of a foot or so on the other side, and the poor vicar had one leg through, with his head protruding, his chin resting on his knee and was unable to move any further as his head was pressed against the top of the hole. He filled the whole aperture and presented such a comic picture, that Frank and I could not assist him, as we had to turn away out of politeness to cover our amusement!

On a later occasion, when Frank and I were at home for the weekend, we, with my three sisters and a cousin, Ruby, decided to attend the morning service at Puxton. We arrived in good time, entered the church and found, as usual, there were no other visitors. We waited for about ten minutes after the service was due to commence, as the vicar had not arrived and then decided to leave, but not before the girls had conscientiously deposited their collection money in the offertory box. However, as we were walking out, we met the vicar with his bicycle coming through the church gate, so we felt obliged to turn back into the church. The vicar followed us in and wheeled his bicycle in and stabled it in the belfry. He then came to us explaining apologetically, that we must not be surprised to find that we were the only members of the congregation. He then retired to the belfry, gave a few tugs on the bell and then emerged, gowned and surpliced and took his place at the reading desk. We went through the complete service of the Book of Common Prayer and recited the Psalms. He played the hymns and eventually ascended the pulpit and gave us a sermon. He then came down and proffered the collection bag, much to the girls discomfiture, and Frank and I were the only ones to make his journey worthwhile!

Altogether it was a very sad situation as the vicar, although regarded as somewhat eccentric, was a man of such high scholarly gifts that the members of a rural community were incapable of appreciating him. This was revealed when an obituary appeared in the London papers, giving a lengthy account of his classical scholarly attainments.

THE COMING OF THE REVEREND C R BLATHWAYT

When the living at Hewish St Anne's was eventually filled the successor to the Revd TA Robinson was the Revd Pizey from Mark, but he was not with us long as he changed livings with the Revd CR Blathwayt and it was the latter who made the greatest impact on the village. He was with us from about 1910-16 and I realise that this gentleman's coming, while not instrumental in all the changes which took place in our parish during his incumbency, seemed to mark them in a manner similar to that of ancient kings in our national history! Some of these changes, then regarded as sensational in the parish, would not in our present age of sophistication provide a talking point for more than a day or two, except among the few immediately concerned.

In a village where there was no big house and no landed gentry, and where the employing class (all farmers) were hardly better educated than their labourers, the Revd Blathwayt stood out as an aristocrat, as indeed he was in manner and bearing.

He was the first vicar who could be regarded as wealthy. A fine handsome figure with a glowing complexion, luxuriant ginger side whiskers, typically Victorian in appearance and general mien. Well built and upright, he walked as if he had the whole world before him and it was his - as the story books say, and with a truly manly stride.

In church, he conducted the services always in an unhurried manner both in speed and movement, which even to me conveyed an impression of dignity and reverence.

Paradoxically, it was the Revd Blathwayt, in spite of his Victorian personality, who brought the age of speed to our parish. With him came not only two or three motor cycles, but a Ford motor car with a resident chauffeur and as far as I can recall, he was the only local car owner we knew until after the First World War! Even our doctor who lived at Banwell, boasted only a motor cycle up to that time but he also had a horse and trap with an attendant groom!

RUNNING BEHIND CARTS

Vicar Blathwayt had not been long in residence when he made a big impact on the children - quite sensational in fact! Coming into school one morning he announced that the practice of running behind carts "Must stop!" Here I should explain that running behind carts was a practice indulged in by most boys and girls, especially if they lived a long distance from school or shops. Hanging on to the back of the cart was often the means of getting to school in good time before the bell stopped, which of course saved a caning or staying in after school. Looking back, I now realise that not only was this a means of getting somewhere much quicker than walking it was exciting, a sport and a challenge with all its attendant thrills!

It was usually a farmer's milk cart going to and from Puxton railway station that helped us on the way to school. As one such passed a group of children there was a wild scramble running after it to hang on to the tailboard and often there was no room for all and it was a running battle to keep one's place and hang on. It was often necessary to know the driver as some would not tolerate hangers on. They flicked their whip behind sometimes playfully, sometimes more viciously.

With drivers like this or with unknown carts, running behind called for a little cunning. As the cart approached one had to look as unconcerned as possible and immediately it passed, make a quick run to catch up and hang on keeping as low as possible to escape detection. A child who could not catch on might shout spitefully to the driver "whip behind!"

It was really great fun if a very fast horse came along! The school or shop would be reached and then one could not let go - that meant being carried along much farther until the horse slowed down a little. We missed no chance to run behind in daylight or dark.

We boys could identify most farmers' carts by the rattle of the cart or the clop-clop of the horses hooves. There were meal drays from Congresbury drawn by two or three horses and those were fine game on the homeward run when empty. One could climb up and ride on the back in comfortable style and well out of the driver's reach. The big furniture vans drawn by little sentinel steam engines provided real treats too and not very speedy. The big tailboards when down were very low and in a level position giving room for many children to climb aboard and ride in comfort.

Now until Vicar Blathwayt arrived, this sport of ours had never been challenged and certainly no one saw any danger in it but to a vicar who frequently rode a motor cycle, the danger was all too apparent and really as other motor vehicles were so few and far between, it might be said that the vicar brought the danger with him! So Vicar Blathwayt, when coming into school one morning, put a different view before us - a lurid picture of a child letting go from a cart and running slap into one of those infernal machines, possibly his, so the game must stop!

His argument alone would not deter us so a bribe was necessary and this was forthcoming in the promise that, if through the year no child was seen "running behind", a day's holiday with an outing, would be our reward! So for two or three years, 1911,12 and 13, we had our reward with an additional outing in the farmers' wagons to Sand Bay where we had tea in a field with sports and games for prizes on the beach. Sand Bay at that time was not developed - there was only a farm down at the far end, no houses or shops along the whole length of the sea front and our teas were provided at the farm house.

On one occasion we went to Max Mills near Winscombe for tea and games on the lawn of a big house belonging to a Miss Buckle who previously lived at Hewish. I remember on that occasion Master Gerald, the vicar's grandson, came and brought with him a beautiful kite which he flew on the lawn. It made me feel envious as our poor efforts were with homemade kites of brown paper, and not only a lovely kite, but a ball of twine seemingly endless. Whereas our twine was made up of various lengths and thicknesses taken from mother's string bag and tied together!

C R BLATHWAYT - NO OUTING - SWINGS REMOVED

As a further incentive Vicar Blathwayt erected a fine pair of swings in the school playground, one for the boys and one for the girls - but at last it happened! Shortly before another outing was due, Vicar Blathwayt came into the school and informed us that as he had seen a boy running behind, there would be no outing! The culprit was not named but we strongly suspected a newcomer to the village. Anyway we fixed on him probably to give our grievance an air of legitimacy!

The swings went too, but for another reason. Vicar Blathwayt came into school on a later occasion profoundly apologetic, explaining that a friend had suggested the possibility of a child becoming seriously injured through falling off a swing, and the further possibility of his being sued for heavy compensation. I remember him saying as he left, "I cannot afford to pay heavy compensation." The ropes were taken down forthwith and later the posts were removed.

Our outings were never restored. The great war broke out, motor traffic increased until the horse and cart was ousted and with it went an innocent sport of our childhood and not the only one in which the highway played an important part.

THE REVD C R BLATHWAYT
- HANDYMAN AND CHURCH LIGHTING

In addition to a chauffeur Vicar Blathwayt employed a cook, a housemaid and one or two handymen for gardening and other outdoor work. Here was change indeed!

The vicarage stable coach house was converted into a garage and workshop, and what a workshop! There were racks and shelves with tools of all descriptions - a tool for every job. For the vicar was a do it yourself man, that is if you excluded the handyman or two who did the spade work and stood by in attendance with the requisite tools. I remember going into the workshop with a message for his Reverence, and was impressed with the array of tools and equipment and he then telling me that he would give the whole outfit to anyone who could name and state the purpose of every tool in the shop! I was then hardly acquainted with anything in the tool line beyond a hammer and pincers, so I was no candidate for such a contest and never likely to be! I think I stood open mouthed in amazement at the thought of such a stupendous offer and that one could make it and stand by it if a successful competitor turned up!

Prior to the coming of Vicar Blathwayt, our church lighting was by means of oil lamps, as it was in most country churches at that time. Our lamps in St Anne's were in groups of three or four fixed to a circular and rather ornate metal frame coloured in blue and gold. Each group was suspended from the roof by a long chain along the centre of the aisle, in the transepts and the chancel. Each lamp had a clear glass chimney with an outer white glass globe - a very poor light compared with modern lighting but as good or better than in the village houses where usually only one good lamp was used in the living room and placed in the centre of the table, while candles sufficed in kitchens and bedrooms.

There was indeed at least one cottage I knew where only candles were used. It was occupied by an old couple who could neither read nor write and the old lady was afraid of oil lamps. In the circumstances candle light was quite sufficient for the old man to sit by the fire enjoying his clay pipe, while the old lady wrapped in several old shawls sat opposite doing all the talking!

This poor lighting in general use, probably explains why beards and side-whiskers were more common with the menfolk. The daily ritual of shaving by candle light with an open razor, to say nothing of the time and skill required to maintain its keen edge, was a very sound reason for using any means to dispense with it! Beards and side-whiskers were certainly the easiest way out! (Safety razors had not come into common use, they were not the efficient article we know today and anyway the renewal of blades was too expensive).

Vicar Blathwayt soon set about an improvement in the church and vicarage by installing an acetylene gas lighting system. This was progress indeed! He also improved his occasional magic lantern shows by extending a pipe across from the church to the school room. These magic lantern shows in winter were real treats to us children - the nearest approach to a thriller! I wonder what the village children would think of such an entertainment today with only an oil lamp in the lantern to throw the slides on the screen, and would they walk a mile or perhaps two on a dark winters night to see it?

I remember a Mr O'Brien was engaged to install the new lighting. A tall imposing gentleman with a military bearing he came from Banwell and went to and fro by bicycle. A small gasometer was erected in the vicarage yard near the coach house or stable and the improved lighting met with widespread approval - particularly no doubt by the sexton, Mr Harry Nichols. One is apt to forget the time and labour involved in preparing for an evening church service in winter. Each lamp had to be kept filled and trimmed, and lighted well before service commenced. It meant the use of a step-ladder to attend to each lamp separately and a similar procedure for extinguishing them after the service. Another good miss too was the smell of paraffin which pervaded the whole building. During winter the church was rarely without the reeking stench. The new gas jets were fixed to the walls at intervals on each side and Vicar Blathwayt was well to the fore with the tools for the job!

After the completion of the installation Mr O'Brien became a regular attendant at our church as a member of the choir and when

Vicar Blathwayt's next innovation was introduced - a surpliced choir - he was appointed choir master. But that is another story in which I may relate an incident, not without a touch of pathos, concerning myself!

The gas lighting served well for many years but became obsolete giving way to electricity, and electric lighting was installed by the generous gift of Mr Harry Jones, a leading farmer in the village and whose family were regular worshippers at our church fifty or so years ago. While this proved a distinct advance and a great improvement over the gas system, I doubt it was greeted with greater enthusiasm, as electric lighting had come into general use in the village and was not such an impressive innovation.

NEW SURPLICED CHOIR

Christmas 1913 was drawing near when Vicar Blathwayt came into the school one morning and informed us that he proposed to have a full surpliced choir of men, women and boys, and their first appearance would be at the Christmas Day service. Additional boys would be required and any desirous of becoming a chorister should present himself at the church on a certain evening that week. I, with about 8 or 9 other boys, attended and our first lesson was a processional walk up and down the aisle. His Reverence was insistent that we walk without swaying and certainly his own bearing was a perfect example. This appeared to be more important than a good voice, as our singing abilities were not questioned then. We sang some Christmas hymns and were each measured for our cassocks.

Several evening practices followed but it seemed to escape the vicar's notice that at these meetings a few more boys came along who had not attended the initial meeting. A few days before Christmas the cassocks and surplices arrived and only then was it revealed to the vicar that the boys outnumbered the cassocks by three!

We boys naturally thought that those who had been measured would be the accepted members - but no! After a brief consultation between the vicar and Mr O'Brien it was announced that the cassocks and surplices should be allotted to the best singers and that six boys of similar size would be tested by singing the first verse of "O come all ye Faithful!"

I was one of the six tested and it came to my turn to sing. "Flat!" announced Mr O'Brien. I would not question his judgement for one moment. I am sure he was right but I was immediately struck by the awful truth that I was out before I was even in and the bitter disappointment found no salve in the fact that we were usurped by two of the latecomers and non-churchgoers at that! I also remember Miss Mary Champion our organist, turning round and offering me a few words of sympathy, this made me want to cry. I went home very dejected and my parents were obviously hurt at my news, especially my mother. (You know how fond mothers are when their dear boys are affronted and my mother was no exception!)

My father called on Vicar Blathwayt and suggested that in the circumstances the system of selection was hardly fair - latecomers, chapel-goers, etc. but the vicar was adamant. Later however, he had second thoughts about my being left out and sent a note to my parents in which he expressed regret, but in view of our family loyalty to the church he felt I should have the honour of being one of the new choir on Christmas Day. If I attended at the vestry in time for the morning service, he would see that I was provided with a surplice and cassock for that service only. I remember the closing words in his note were something like this. "If his voice is below standard, he must sing small!"

At first, I was reluctant to take this offer wondering how a surplice and cassock could be provided for one service only, but I eventually decided to accept thinking that the possibility of an extra surplice and cassock being provided might make me a permanent chorister after all!

I arrived in good time for the service, much to the surprise of the other boys who were soon robed and in processional order with the ladies and girls in surplices and mortar boards - a sensational innovation this for a village choir - and then the men. They all assembled in the north transept where the organ now stands, the transept being curtained off and the curtains were drawn to and fro by a system of cords and pulleys (another product of the vicar's inventive mind). He was about to draw the curtains and announce the processional hymn when his eyes fell on me sitting very self-concious and feeling decidedly uncomfortable. He forthwith told one of the boys to take off his cassock and surplice and give them to me, curtly explaining his promise. I remember feeling sorry for the boy concerned, he had to sit in the vestry throughout the service and understandably this did not please his parents either when he did not appear in the procession! A very sorry and rather distasteful affair altogether.

But a little consolation came my way when we returned to school after the holidays. Our headmaster, Mr Farr, who too was a chorister, was away throughout Christmas and was not aware of all this, but he noticed I was not in the choir on the Sunday after his return. On the Monday morning in class he said "Hey M!" (he addressed me by my nickname, as was his habit with all the boys who proudly answered to one - uncomplimentary though some of them were - including mine!). "Why wern't you in the choir yesterday?" I replied with a break in my voice, "Because I sing flat sir". "Oh" says Mr Farr, "that's nothing! Most of 'em do!" Rightly or wrongly I took certain comfort from that. My banishment however did not last long as the novelty of being a chorister soon lost its edge with some of the boys and I was able to take the place of an absentee Sunday after Sunday. Presumably I still sung flat, maybe I still do, but with Mr Farr's words in mind, I was not unduly concerned about such a trifling matter.

THE SINGLE CHURCH BELL

Prior to 1912 the church possessed only one bell. It was the intention when the church was built in 1864 to include a tower to house a full peal, but in the course of erection it collapsed. The nature of the soil and the vibration of passing trains nearby precluded the building of a tower substantial enough to carry the weight. So it was decided to erect a tiny turret in the corner of the north transept capable of housing one solitary bell. It was rung for about five minutes by the sexton before every service and also always at 8 o'clock every Sabbath morning to remind parishioners of the time, to ensure their being ready in time for the morning service at 11 am.

It should be recalled that no-one had the correct time in their homes. There being no means of checking for Greenwich Mean Time - and for all local purposes a variation of a quarter of an hour or so was of no great importance. I recall that the old sexton often called at the railway signal box on Saturday evenings to put his watch right for the 8 o'clock bell - this being the only place where GMT was recorded.

It was a common thing too for villagers who were going somewhere by train (a rare occurrence) to ascertain the correct time by the same means before setting out on the 2½ mile walk to Puxton station.

THE PASSING BELL

It was another important duty of the sexton to toll the passing bell as soon as possible after the death of a parishioner. It being regarded as a solemn duty for a bereaved member of the family to inform the sexton, who lost no time in going to the tower to toll the bell. What a solemn sonorous note it was - there was a long pause between each pull of the rope. The ringer, it was said waited for the sound to die away between each ring. There was a code too, I understand, to indicate whether the deceased was a man, woman or child - a certain number of rings in quick succession before the solemn toll commenced.

As soon as it became known for whom the bell tolled all villagers acquainted with the deceased immediately drew their blinds as a mark of respect, and, in the case of near friends and relatives, they remained drawn until after the funeral.

The parish did not possess a bier and although an occasional horse-drawn hearse was seen to pass through the village containing a coffin for burial somewhere distant, the hire of the hearse from Bristol was out of the question on grounds of expense and all coffins were borne on the shoulders of local bearers (usually neighbours) from the house of the deceased to the churchyard, and followed by mourners on foot. In one or two exceptional cases, owing to distance and the deceased being a heavy weight, the parish bier from Congresbury was borrowed by the undertaker, who pushed it down the two and a half miles. At the churchyard during the interment the bell was solemnly tolled.

TUBULAR BELLS

Vicar Blathwayt, however, decided that our church merited something better than a solitary bell. A peal of real bells being out of the question, he had the idea of the next best thing - tubular bells! These could be easily accommodated in the existing small tower, so the vicar called a meeting in the school room to discuss the matter with the elders of the church. Details were given with an estimated cost which the vicar had obtained and I believe the figure was £197.10s - no small sum in those days for a tiny parish to muster. All present seemed in favour so the vicar invited subscriptions. I was allowed to attend this, my first public meeting - now 12 years old, and if my memory is not at fault, the vicar headed the list with £50, this was followed by promises of £10 down to one pound by those present, but the sum was far from the required amount.

It was however decided to have the bells and the vicar lost no time in placing an order with Messrs Harringtons of Coventry. Shortly afterwards another meeting was called when the vicar announced that a fund existed under the will of one Mary Pardoe, whereby the bells would be paid for. The one condition being that any parish taking advantage of this benefaction should place a memorial tablet recording the gift and the name of the donor in a suitable position in or near the tower. Such a condition could of course be easily complied with and so St Anne's had its bells free of cost. The tablet was duly fixed in the church and the would-be subscribers kept their money. I believe the information relating to Mary Pardoe's legacy came from the makers after the order was placed.

It was a great day when the bells rang out for the first time, but the occasion did not pass without criticism, mainly by those who expected to hear the rich heavy resonant tones similar to those heard from the neighbouring parishes of Congresbury, Yatton and Wrington. All of which could be heard in turn on a very still night.

My father and his colleague were the first to ring the bells, and the novelty attracted others too for a while but it was left to father and Mr Bailey to ring for all occasions, sometimes together and sometimes singly. The eight ropes were fixed in a chiming frame. They translated a selection of hymns from the tune books to numbers until they had a good selection which was within the compass of one scale and also on occasion they simulated a muffled peal by a very light pull on the ropes. Occasionally the vicar visited the tower and had a go.

I have a very pleasant memory of accompanying them both on New Year's Eve in 1913, I think at midnight, to ring out the old year and on the way home stopping to listen to neighbouring bells. It was a very quiet night and how lovely they sounded - probably Yatton, Congresbury and/or Kingston Seymour or Wick St Lawrence. They were very happy days for a village schoolboy, now more appreciated in retrospect.

CHURCH CLOSURE

Now in 1979, on 9 September, Hewish church was closed owing to lack of support and as a member of one of the oldest families of worshippers there (from 1898 to 1935) I was privileged to read the last lesson at the last service held there, when the church had a very full attendance.

The centenary of the church was celebrated in 1965 and to mark the occasion and as a tribute to the memory of our parents, we my brother and sisters, paid for the bells to be restored as they had been out of action for some time. A metal plaque recording our gift was fixed in the church. Shortly after the closure in 1979 the bells were stolen and I was given the plaque together with the family pew, which we regularly occupied at the service.

GOODING DAY

The 21 December (St Thomas's Day) was known locally as Gooding Day. All the poorer children absented themselves from school to go "Gooding". They went to the farmers houses around the district as far as Rolstone, Wick St Lawrence and along the Nye Road to Sandford asking for "something for Christmas". They each carried a sack and were usually given apples or a few coppers and perhaps an occasional orange. One or two farmers' wives who were more generously inclined, prepared for their visits by making a batch of cakes and giving out two or three to each child. We children who did not go "Gooding" of course, attended school as usual and we too looked forward to Gooding Day as there was such a sparse attendance that no lessons were done and we had a long playtime in the playground.

When Mr Gowar arrived as schoolmaster, about 1910, he organised indoor games for us although he was very scathing about the poor attendance and sarcastically referred to Gooding Day as Begging Day! He was exceptionally keen on a good attendance and was most anxious to record a 100% attendance for a whole week, promising a day's holiday should this be achieved - but we never made it during his tenure.

I felt his attitude was unjust and lacked sympathy for the Gooders, in most cases it was probably the only Christmas fare to come their way. He was a city man and failed to appreciate that Gooding Day was an age old custom in our village.

CONGRESBURY FAIR

Another day which we who attended school enjoyed, was when Congresbury Fair came around on a day in September. Most of the farmers' children stayed away from school for this and many other children beside went to the fair, though with little or no money to spend they walked to Congresbury for the sheer excitement. I would have liked to have been one of them, but my parents would not allow us to miss a day at school for such an event.

OTHER GAMES

Another game which came around in season was conkers and as there were two conker trees in the field alongside the road on our way to school, we were always able to maintain a supply while the season lasted.

We carried a horseshoe nail to bore a hole through the centre of the horse chestnut. Threading it on a short length of string we then took it in turns with another player to try to smash each others conker. One player held his conker out at arm's length suspended on the string for his opponent to swing his conker in an attempt to smash it. For every conker smashed the victor's was credited with "one year old" and if one boasted of a conker being 9 or 10 years old when it was eventually smashed, the victor added that number to his conker. It was generally frowned upon as cheating when one baked a conker in the oven to harden it, but most of us did it!

Following the close of the conker season in late Autumn was hoop bowling. The boys always had iron hoops and the girls wooden ones. The latter were much bigger than the boys' iron hoops and were bowled with a stick and the girls used to run in and out of theirs as they went along, but the boys' hoops were bowled and controlled with a wire hook, though hoops were never taken to school. Not many boys had real iron hoops, they occasionally improvised with an iron band of a barrel but they were shaped to fit the barrel consequently were biased and could not be bowled straight. Others sometimes used the rim of an old bicycle or pram wheel.

With all the games throughout the year each had its season which did not deviate from year to year. Each game was always played at about the same time each year and they followed in regular sequence; marbles, whip-tops, hoops and skipping ropes, conkers, etc. None of them seemed to overlap and as each season ended the next game seemed suddenly to appear. The previous ones quickly faded out and was not seen again until the following year. There were, of course, all the year round pursuits - ring games, rounders, hop-scotch by the girls, hares and hounds and football or cricket after school hours.

BICYCLES

Only two boys possessed bicycles and the lucky owner of one of these was the vicar's grandson - "Master Gerald" as we were expected to call him! He was about eleven years of age and his bicycle was a gleaming new machine. How we envied him and gazed in awe whenever he passed us. The other cycle was owned by a schoolboy of similar age - his machine was far from new-looking as it was given him by a distant relative who had outgrown it, but he too created feelings of envy.

Not many men owned a bicycle in spite of the fact that some of them had to walk a good distance to and from their place of work. Our family acquired an old one discarded by an aunt. It was a lady's model a Rudge Whitworth and it was said that it was the first lady's cycle seen in her village - Ide, near Exeter, when she was in her teens. It was, of course, regarded as my mother's but she could not ride it until she had had some lessons. My father had to accompany her by walking beside her until she had learnt to ride it. This may sound strange today but it was by no means an uncommon sight to see a man or woman taking lessons in this manner. Mother had several lessons before she could steer and then the next stage was to balance without the aid of Father holding the saddle. The first time this was done the pupil was not informed until he or she had ridden forward for a few yards unaided, then the teacher shouted "you are riding by yourself" and in mother's case I believe as soon as she heard that she immediately fell off! It was also remarkable that a learner often could not resist riding straight towards an obstacle even with plenty of room in which to pass it. Mother eventually became proficient and was able to cycle to Weston, shopping. One fails to realise what a boon this was, remembering there were no buses and a journey by train to Weston super Mare involved a 2½ mile walk to Puxton station.

The vicar also got around on a motor cycle with a basket chair type of trailer attached and he was often seen riding through the village with his wife as a passenger. It was said that on more than one occasion the trailer turned over and tipped the good lady on to the road. Mrs Jones, who died recently at Congresbury, was a domestic servant at the vicarage and she told me that occasionally she was taken in the trailer on an errand to Weston. It was either a very dusty ride or a very muddy one as the roads at that time were not tarmacked and she rode either in a cloud of dust or a shower of mud thrown up by the motor cycle! In the summer the limestone surface created such a cloud of dust that the hedges and the grass verges were completely white. Along the sides of the roads there was almost an inch of white powdered limestone and one could not walk very far without one's clothes and shoes becoming completely covered. Folks living along the roadside were obliged to keep their doors and windows closed during a spell of dry weather.

In wet weather pools of water filled the pot holes of which there were many in the cart wheel tracks and the thick layer of dust became a coating of mud. The metal tyres of carts and wagons ground all the loose limestone into dust. There were no rubber tyres then except on the small governess pony carts which many farmers used to take their wives to Weston on shopping expeditions or social visits.

In winter when the roads became so muddy a road scraper was brought into use - it was horse-drawn with the driver walking behind with the reins. The scraper unit was about half the width of the road and was composed of narrow scraper blades fitted closely together each working independently to rise or fall according to the uneven surface of the road. It was fixed in a slanting position which caused the mud collected to run to the roadside and it formed a shallow ridge of mud along the grass verge.

When the pot holes became numerous and some of them fairly deep, they were filled in by a man with a puttload of limestones. They were tipped into the holes loosely but were soon ground to powder by the farmers carts and wagons which only added to the dust or mud according to the weather. A putt was a heavy two-wheeled cart used for general haulage. Occasionally during the summer a horse-drawn water cart passed through the village spraying water at the rear to lay the dust.

SCHOOL ABSENCES

There were two seasons when absences from school were more frequent - at gardening time in the Spring and for blackberrying in the Autumn. The soil at Hewish was mainly of heavy clay and when first dug in the Spring the surface was a mass of large heavy lumps which could not be broken down while wet into a fine tilth. They were left to dry out when they became baked hard - then they were smashed by hard hitting with a long handled wooden mallet. For this task many labourers' sons were kept home from school and their reason give to the school master for their absence was "Please sir, I had to maul the clumps abroad". I remember the puzzled look on a new school master's face when offered this reason on the first occasion. It seemed a very valid one when one remembers the limited time their fathers had to complete the digging prior to "tater" planting. Coming home from work at 6 pm after milking time, their gardening time was very limited and often a spell of wet weather put them behind with planting.

WATERY GRAVES

The ground at Hewish was very water-logged. There were no springs anywhere in the village and for a water supply many farms had their own well, but it was only surface water that drained into them. For this reason when a grave was dug in the churchyard, it often became almost half-filled with water during the funeral service and the grave diggers were kept busy dipping out the water with long handled dipping bowls to keep it as shallow as possible when the coffin was lowered. Occasionally they scattered laurel leaves down on the surface in an effort to conceal the water from the mourners.

BLACKBERRY SEASON

Owing to frequent absences at blackberry time we always had one week's holiday when the season was at its height, but many stayed from school before and after the holiday. For this was the only occasion when the children were able to make a little money. A man came from Weston on Mondays, Wednesdays and Fridays with a light pony-drawn wagon covered with a rounded canvas, like a small gipsy caravan. At the first picking he, Mr Cousins, paid twopence per pound but as blackberries became more plentiful he paid a 1½ d and then 1d per pound. Later they dropped to three farthings and finally to a halfpenny, but we stopped picking at that price. Many women went out picking all day carrying two buckets. Another purchaser came from Congresbury, Mr George Poultney, and he kept us supplied with chip baskets.

The Weston man was a surly fellow and according to him our pickings were always a pound or so less than we made them on our scales at home, much to our disguSt. But we could do nothing about it as we always left ours at the Full Quart Inn, which was his collecting point while we were at school. I remember earning eleven shillings at one season - a real fortune! This must have been in 1912 as my brother Harold, then 15, was a lad porter on the GWR at Wookey Station near Wells. He was earning 12s per week out of which he paid 10s per week for lodgings (50p in new money), consequently mother had to assist him in his upkeep of clothes. At that time she was about to make him some shirts and mother persuaded me to give a big share of my blackberry money towards the cost of Harold's shirting material. I grudgingly consented, no doubt through mother's pleadings. I realise now that she was having a tough time financially. She had fitted Harold out with new clothes on his going away from home and with four growing children around her it was a severe strain on her housekeeping expenses. But when Harold came home for the weekend, once a fortnight, I did not hesitate to remind him frequently that I paid for his shirts out of my blackberry money!

POSTAL SERVICES

During my earlier years we had one postal delivery daily, including Sundays, but later two deliveries were made. The morning mail was thrown from the mail train passing through in the early hours at 60-70 miles per hour. There was erected at the side of the railway line, about a quarter of a mile below the church and school, the mail apparatus. It consisted of a very strong rope net which had to be opened out by the postman prior to the train's passing time and then folded back and securely locked after picking up the mail, which was in a large heavy leather bag bound and secured with very thick leather straps. As the train approached, the men on the train extended the mail bag by swinging it out on a hooked jib, which when arrested by the open net, was thrown into it with terrific force and in the evening the outgoing mail was taken to the same site in the great leather bag in which the morning mail arrived, and the same operation was effected but in reverse.

This was common practice at many places along the line. There was a similar apparatus at Yatton and that bag contained the mail for outlying villages including Congresbury. The mail was brought to Congresbury Post Office by a horse-drawn van and the postmen for the outlying villages came there to collect the appropriate bag for their area and took it to their Post Office for sorting and subsequent delivery. When an afternoon delivery was introduced later the Hewish postman cycled to Congresbury to collect it.

TELEGRAMS

There being no telephone in the village, any urgent communications were by telegram. I believe a telegram cost sixpence or a shilling for a fixed number of words and any words in excess were charged extra at so much each word, probably a halfpenny or penny. Telegrams were transmitted to and from Congresbury by the morse code and incoming telegrams for Hewish were delivered by a messenger on a bicycle. The method was used only in extreme emergencies, often in the case of a villager being informed of the death of a relative. Indeed when the messenger was seen cycling through the village folks began to surmise whose death it might be! As telegrams usually conveyed bad news, recipients often opened them full of trepidation. The idea of sending a greetings telegram had not caught on in those years, it was too expensive for ordinary village folk.

POVERTY

It must be remembered that poverty was rife in the village as most of the residents were farm labourers and their wages were extremely low - from about 16 or 18 shillings per week. In this respect it was no worse than in any other rural community, consequently many children were ill shod and poorly clothed. I recall one family in particular where the boys looked half starved and their mother often wrote a note to my mother. It was often written on a scrap of brown paper or on a piece torn off the wall and was almost unreadable. It usually contained a request for any of mine or my brother's left off clothes or a pair of boots which we may have grown out of. I also have a vivid memory of her oldest boy, who was about my age, coming away from the village shop one evening and I with another boy met him and our usual greeting when meeting a schoolmate was to ask where he had been and what for. In this case he had been for a pennyworth of bacon for his father's evening meal and it was just one rasher. He had bitten a piece out of it and was smoothing out the teethmarks! He could not speak plainly and on one occasion arrived very late for school and when asked for an explanation he said "I had to go down to the fop for some foap" (shop for some soap). This caused much amusement to the other boys who cruelly mocked him "Fop for some foap".

During very cold wet weather, he often came to us to borrow my "trucks" to fetch some coal from Congresbury (3 miles distant). This meant absence from school for the morning and when he arrived in the afternoon he was cold, obviously wet through and was severely rebuked for not bringing a note to explain his absence in the morning. Now my trucks was a large wooden sugar box on a pair of old pram wheels with a pair of shafts. We used it mainly to play horses and carts and I often gave my little sister, Ena, rides in it. We used it too for scrumping apples in the orchard down our lane. It was my favourite and only big toy and I often scrubbed it out to keep it clean, consequently, when poor Gilbert returned it I was angry to see the interior wet and black from the coal carrying. My mother severely remarked "Think yourself lucky that you don't have to walk to Congresbury in the wet to fetch just a half-hundred weight of coal!" (56 lbs). At that time about nine pennyworth (old money).

There was a labourer in the village called, Oliver Hewlett, but Gilbert could only refer to him as "Olliyujah" and thereafter we always referred to Oliver as "Olliyujah" - out of grown ups hearing of course. His father was very crippled and worked on a farm. It was said that on account of his disability he was paid much less then an able-bodied man.

Very few children had money to spend on sweets and when a child produced some sweets during playtime, others gathered around, begging for one. Oranges were only available around Christmas time and when a lad had one at playtime others begged him for a piece of it, and if it was not forthcoming he was asked for the peel, which some boys eagerly devoured. Similarly when the apple season was over and a lad had an apple, he was begged to "give us a bite," and if this was refused "give us the core then!"

THE POOR MAN AT HIS GATE

One very cold hard winter, 1912 or 13, Vicar Blathwayt became conscious of the hardships of many of his parishioners and he ordered the coal merchant to deliver two hundredweights to all residents other than farmers and trades people, followed up with a pair of blankets under the same conditions. Evidently as we were regarded as better off than the farm labourers, Mrs Blathwayt called on mother and tactfully asked if she would be offended to take advantage of this unexpected bounty. Of course mother said she would be pleased to accept - delighted in fact. No doubt it was a real godsend to poor Gilbert's family and it saved the poor lad a few journeys to Congresbury with my borrowed trucks for a while.

DEATH OF TWINS

There was a farm labourer with a big family and obviously they were very poor in consequence. The children were undernourished and under sized. About this time, 1912/13, their two youngest children, twins, commenced school at five years of age and these toddlers had to walk nearly two miles. They lived in a tiny cottage on the way to Rolstone. It was a cold wet period when they commenced schooling and within a week or two, one died of pneumonia. Within another couple of weeks, the other died. They were buried at Banwell and I remember we took coppers to school to provide wreaths.

CHRISTMAS

Our Christmas celebrations at home were very exciting to us children - especially the anticipation during the week or two before. It began, I think, when we commenced singing carols at school and we particularly liked Good King Wenceslas. Then we heard that our only sweet shop had some Christmas goodies on show at the Post Office. It seemed quite exciting, although it consisted only of one small showcase at the end of the counter which contained a few Christmas stockings made of net material in which one could see a pink sugar mouse and a few other small items. They cost one penny or twopence each but we never bought one as they were considered expensive and a waste of money - in any case we had none. But one or two children who had money to spend brought one to school. The shop was not decorated but that showcase was another reminder that Christmas was coming.

Then at home mother commenced making her Christmas puddings and in the evenings we sat around the kitchen table, stoning the raisins and of course slyly popping one into our mouths. Mother made up her own mincemeat for the mince pies and tarts. Most people did in those days and just the sight of all the sultanas, currants, lemon peel and other ingredients covering the table, tended to add to our excitement. Then, when all was ready, she mixed the ingredients for the puddings in a large earthenware bowl and it was most important that every member of the family had to have a stir - which was quite a ceremony in itself.

Not the least of the important duties which mother had to undertake was the boiling of the Christmas puddings. Mother usually made eight or nine and the one for consumption on Christmas Day was in the largest basin and had the precious silver threepenny piece embedded in it. The puddings had to be boiled for either eight or twelve hours (I am not sure which) but it was important to maintain them continuously at boiling point. So as the water boiled away it had to be carefully topped up at intervals and the fire maintained underneath.

There was always one in a very tiny basin which was a "taster" to sample as soon as it was cold. During the process of boiling, the house was full of steam and with a smell quite different from that on the weekly washing day - not unpleasant and quite a seasonable odour!

Our father was a Devonshire man and in his younger days lived with an uncle in a remote farmstead, where an important part of their Christmas festivities commenced on Christmas Eve with the burning of the ashen faggot. It was of course made of ash wood - a large bundle secured around with several bonds of withy and it was the custom to pass the cider mug around every time a bond snapped. At the old farmhouses they had huge open hearth fireplaces, in which they could burn a huge faggot, but father had to be content with a very small bundle for our tiny fireplace and it had to be kept in place by fixing the poker upright in front of it. Christmas would not have been complete for father without his ashen faggot and he always had a four and a half gallon cask of cider for the occasion.

Then of course, we had to hang up our stockings and long before it was time to get up we would grab them off the bedpost at the foot of the bed and commence groping in the contents. How exciting it was! There was usually an orange right down in the toe and a few nuts and sweets, perhaps a cracker and then the "piece de resistance". Of course we knew what that would be for had we not made our requests known to Santa Claus long before, by shouting up the chimney? One Christmas my choice was a pocket knife with two blades, and all I could do until we got up was to finger it fondly and keep opening and shutting the blades. On the way to church (we always attended the Christmas morning service) I cut a stick from the hedgerow and carved out notches in it as I walked along. Had it been Sunday this would have been forbidden but Christmas Day was on a weekday that year.

How exciting it all was, but it lost some of its glamour when, as we got older, we learnt the truth about Santa Claus. It was quite a shock and a great disappointment, but we still hung up our stockings and it was still great fun. At a later Christmas, my chief gift was an electric torch. It was a flat one with a huge bulls eye lens - they cost about one shilling (5p). I was particularly proud of this as only one other boy at school possessed one. At that time they were considered only as toys and grown ups never used them. The oil burning hurricane lantern was the main outdoor lighting for farmers getting around the farm buildings and in the milking sheds, while nervous old ladies carried a little candle lantern to and from church or chapel.

CHRISTMAS TREES

We never had a Christmas tree - they had not become fashionable and were only seen at Sunday School Christmas treats. They were not used in villagers' cottages, no doubt mainly because it meant duplicating the Christmas presents which could not be afforded. Also through being lit up with tiny candles and decorated with tinsel, it presented a grave fire risk. Anyway we children felt that a tree would be no substitute for the magic of our Christmas stocking.

The next thrill on Christmas day was our dinner and the thought of the silver three penny piece hidden in the "pudden". In whose helping would it be found? As dinner time grew near our eager anticipation became exciting! Of course mother and father might get it - that would be just too bad! After all they had plenty of money! The procedure was for mother to announce for whom the next helping would be, as sometimes the wonderful coin could be seen and fell out, so it was dealt with in order of our ages. It was like winning the Pools, or a Premium Bond today!

After dinner we had nuts and ginger wine and crackers. Crackers were disappointing as their contents were tawdry or useless, but it was all part of our Christmas. Also we had a fire in our big front room and we stayed up and had a proper supper - that too was a special treat. Mother and father joined us in the fireside games in the evening - Blind Man's Buff, Spinning the Trencher and Hidey Stick in the Dark Hole - and when we were quite small father was a bear or an elephant and gave us rides on all fours.

We never had turkey or goose for our Christmas dinner as father always fattened one of his cockerels and this was supplemented by a large joint of beef, which always tasted nicer than any we had throughout the year.

During Christmas week we had three or four of our school friends in to tea, when we also played the usual fireside games throughout the afternoon and evening. Then the compliment was returned and we spent another evening at our neighbours' with tea and games. Our teas then were always something special, with iced Christmas cake and mince pies. It seemed always to be the custom for our mothers to exchange a sample of their "Christmas pudden".

Oranges too were another feature of our Christmas. Mother ordered some with her fortnightly delivery of groceries for a while after Christmas. I don't think they were available all the year round as they are now. A young shop assistant came around on alternate Mondays for orders and all our groceries were delivered later in the week.

My parents were very keen Co-op members and rarely bought anything from the local shop and post office, which was kept by Mr H Light. The Co-op dividend was the attraction. Most of the more thrifty members of the working class dealt with the Co-op and when in 1914 my father had his house built, the accumulated "divi" was sufficient to pay for the land (£40.00 I think) and a mortgage was taken out with the Co-op for the building of the house - that was at Homelea on the main road a little way below the Palmer's Elm Inn.

The groceries were delivered by horse and van. One memorable occasion was when the man came with our groceries a day or two before Christmas and on account of the heavy deliveries he arrived late in the evening. Ours was the only delivery down our lane at the Railway Crossing house so he always turned his horse and cart around in the field gateway, just over the bridge spanning the rhine. On this occasion he took out our box of groceries and had to bring them back over the bridge to come into our gate. Unfortunately, he went on the outside of the bridge railings and slipped down over the bank into the water and had a real ducking while some of our groceries floated away downstream! It was a dark and filthy night and obviously the man was in a sorry plight when he came to the door - wet through and covered in slimy mud! Mother fixed him up with dry clothes and a warm drink. Fortunately I think ours was the last delivery on his round.

The next morning brother Harold and I walked down the bank of the rhine and recovered one or two items stopped against the hatch about a quarter of a mile below. I remember a packet of matches (a dozen boxes) floating out of our reach but they would have been quite useless.

Copy of a Christmas Carol

Composed by the Revd C R Blathwayt
Vicar of St Anne's, Hewish, 1911-16

THE CHRISTMAS ANGELS
A MULTITUDE OF THE HEAVENLY HOST

Bright angel wings across the sky
Sweep on with swift melodious flight,
And deathless words that cannot die,
Peal softly through the tranquil night.

Calm soothing tones to man forlorn,
Then, striking full redemption's chord,
"Rejoice! for unto you is born
A Saviour who is Christ the Lord",

O ye who sang this sweet refrain
To shepherds under Bethlehem's sky
Reveal yourselves to us again,
And lead us to the Christ on high.

Let now your tuneful voices ring,
And bid earth's weary discord cease,
Ye herald messengers! O! sing,
The Advent of the Prince of Peace.

That we who daily wage the war
With sin, in all its darksome guise;
To purer heights with you may soar
And learn the music of the skies.

AMEN

C R B. December 1887.

Sung to the tune of "Jesus shall reign where 'er the sun".

BUTCHER

We had only one meat delivery each week. Butcher Tucker came on Fridays from Milton with his horse and van and mother bought the Sunday joint and sufficient meat to last through the rest of the week. Looking back it amazes us how mother managed without a fridge. The butcher also had no such facility, but I believe they packed their meat around with large blocks of ice supplied by a local ice-factory. We had a small larder just outside the back door in which was a meat-safe - (a cupboard with door and sides of perforated zinc - where it was fairly cool and fly-proof). Mother used to go out to Butcher Tucker's van and look over various joints hung all around the sides, select her joint and then haggle over the price. How housewives used to haggle over a penny or half-penny. It was common practice and reveals how every copper counted in their housekeeping budgets. The butcher was the victim of many a woman's sharp tongue on his next visit if the joint last week proved tough!

On one of these occasions, while the butcher went into the house to purchase our eggs, I asked his permission to turn his horse around and drive the van back over the crossing. On arriving on the other side a fire was burning in the adjoining orchard and the smoke wafting across the road frightened the horse. It started going backwards and the wheels turned so that the van was across the road. It continued backing and I could not control it until the back of the van dropped over the bank into the ditch, leaving the horse and front wheels on the grass verge. The doors at the back flew open and eggs which the butcher had previously purchased from other customers rolled out into the ditch along with sundry small articles. Needless to say, I was very frightened but by the time the alarm was raised it was time to go back to school and I escaped the wrath of Butcher Tucker and my parents. He was very tolerant and I did not receive a reprimand when next he called. The gang of railway men working on the permanent way nearby soon heaved the van out and no further damage was caused.

RUNNING ERRANDS FOR MOTHER - THE BAKER

Our bread was delivered on Mondays, Wednesdays and Fridays from Mr Nicholls' bakery in Broad Street, Congresbury. The shop is now a small grocery business managed by Mr & Mrs Frank Wyatt on mini-market lines.

I remember once mother found she required more bread over the weekend and on the Saturday afternoon I had to walk up to Congresbury (about 2½ miles) for an extra loaf or two. Not an errand which attracted me on a fine sunny afternoon, but Mrs Nicholls, a motherly soul, no doubt sympathised at the long hot dusty walk and gave me a few sweets in a bag. This was such a real treat, I felt the long wearisome walk was worthwhile.

OTHER VISITS TO CONGRESBURY

We rarely had occasion to make any visits to Congresbury during our school days. When about twelve years of age I walked up to the Post Office one evening after school to deposit the sum of one shilling (5 new pence) in the post office savings bank. At that time a form was provided on which were spaces to affix twelve penny postage stamps and now over a long period I completed the form with my last penny. It became necessary for me to go to Congresbury as the post Office at Hewish did not handle savings bank business. The Post Offices then were kept open until quite late in the evening.

I also remember taking a day off from haymaking with Farmer Jones, to cycle to Congresbury with mother and catch a train to Cheddar, to join up with a large party from Weston organised by the local Cooperative Society, on a days outing visiting the caves and then having sports and running races in a field near the station.

A couple of years later I cycled up to purchase a new battery (costing three old pence) for my electric torch given me for Christmas and mentioned earlier.

STALE BREAD

We never ate new bread in our family, it was considered bad for the digestion, but sometimes we were out of stale bread and then mother used to send us up to a friendly neighbour (Mrs Neath) with a new loaf and a request to exchange it for a stale one.

On one occasion I was sent on this errand, with our new loaf wrapped in a sheet of newspaper. When I reached the top of our lane a hay cart was passing, so here was an opportunity to run behind in the manner I have already related and if possible get a ride. It was a two wheeled hay cart returning empty. Now a hay cart consisted of a slatted floor with no sides or back - it sloped to the centre slightly from the ends and sides like a large elongated, shallow dish. The cart was higher than my shoulder so to hang on with both hands I placed the loaf on the wagon and with the steady jogging of the horse my loaf was soon out of the newspaper, dancing and bouncing all over the wagon and inclined to the centre, well out of my reach, of course. Now I had to clamber up on the cart to retrieve it and at one time it danced right up under the driver's seat. It was a difficult operation and by the time I got on the wagon and crawled up towards the driver to grab the loaf we were well past Mrs Neath's house and when I got down on to the road again clutching the loaf, minus the newspaper, I was about a quarter of a mile beyond! The sight of the loaf dancing over the wagon tickled me immensely. I could not help laughing and when Mrs Neath came to the door I burst into such a loud fit of laughter that I could not speak. This behaviour obviously embarrassed her as she thought I was laughing at her. When she next met mother she told her about it and I was severely rebuked for my rudeness!

HARD WORKING MOTHER

We do not realise what a hard life it was for working class mothers, just drudgery from Monday morning to Saturday night and there was hardly any respite on Sunday, with a traditional Sunday roast dinner to prepare. How trying this must have been in the summer, over a hot kitchen range, with two or three saucepans boiling on top and a fire to be frequently stoked up, necessitating the removal of the saucepans to replenish the fire. The saucepans were of iron and very heavy, as aluminium was then unknown and the washing up entailed the removal of a coating of soot on the bottom of each article. I realise now what a chore this must have been, with a limited supply of hot water and no washing up liquids or powders, as we use today. Mother managed though to clean up and take a short rest before tea, when she read her weekly magazine - "The Sunday Companion" and on Monday she exchanged it for the "Lady's Companion" with our neighbour, Mrs Neath.

The magazines were delivered Saturdays by a newsagent Mr Robbins who came on foot from Worle also bringing the local weeklies - the Weston Mercury and the Weston Gazette. These were the only newspapers available and most householders bought a copy of one of them (the former was a Conservative and the latter a Liberal publication). We took the Liberal one, it being in line with my father's strong convictions.

MOTHER'S LABOUR SAVERS
- THE SEWING MACHINE AND THE MANGLE

The only implements which mother had to ease her lot were a treadle Singer sewing machine and a heavy mangle or clothes wringer and every weekday evening it seemed to me that she spent it making or mending. She made Harold and me weekday clothes for school. We wore knickerbockers which buttoned or buckled below the knee, and long black stockings. Our Sunday suits were bought ready-made and of course there was much handing down from Harold when he grew out of a suit. Much of the girls clothes were also made by mother and I often remember falling asleep hearing her working her treadle downstairs. I remember too the pile of stockings she had to darn generally on Friday or Saturday nights. These were neither nylon nor similar hard wearing materials and we were very heavy on our stockings.

The mangle too was a great boon for mother on washing days, always on a Monday. The copper boiler had to be filled with buckets of water carried in from the rainwater butts or when they were empty during a dry spell, dipped from the rhine alongside the yard, where some rough steps were cut out of the banks down to the water's edge. The copper fire had to be maintained, the ashes taken out and the water dipped out by a dipping bowl when the washing was finished. During the whole process the scullery was full of steam and the door leading into the kitchen had to be kept closed.

Now the mangle was quite a heavy and bulky piece of machinery, a large cast iron frame in which were fitted two wooden rollers five or six inches in diameter and the pressure between them could be adjusted by a leaf spring, regulated by a screw which was turned at the top. (The rubber rollers of much smaller diameter had not yet become available.) The machine was between 4 and 5 feet in height, was very heavy (about 1½ or 2 cwts) and took up quite a lot of room. It was a real labour saver for mother though and in addition to wringing the wet clothes she was able to press and fold her sheets by screwing down the rollers more tightly and thus save ironing.

The copper fire referred to above consisted of a large basin-like copper container of six or seven gallons capacity, embedded in a brick built structure over a fire box. It was an essential unit to be found in every house and was usually built in a corner of the scullery. In it the weekly wash was boiled and the water on bath nights each Friday, also the Christmas puddings. It was surmounted by a wooden cover. Also to be found with every house was a large water butt situated near the back door to catch the rain water off the roof. Both the items were the duty of the landlord to provide as was also the privy, usually erected at the far end of the garden, built of brick or stone, usually over a cesspit but sometimes with just a bucket beneath the seat.

SATURDAYS

On Saturday mornings we sometimes had to take a turn cleaning the table knives. They were of ordinary steel (not stainless - this did not exist at the time). We had to scour them by rubbing the blades briskly to and fro on a broad board over which we sprinkled powdered bath brick. "Bath bricks" was the general scouring agent at the time. It was sold in the shape of bricks and was a product of a sediment found only in the river at Bridgwater. It was first produced by a man named Bath, hence its name and was brownish yellow in colour, but is now no longer available as so many varieties of proprietary cleaning agents have come on the market which are more efficient and call for less energy.

Until my brother Harold left home, most Saturdays for me were fairly free except occasionally when we had a couple of pigs. They were turned out into the lane to rout about on the grass verges and I had to stay and keep an eye on them, for which father sometimes gave me a half-penny! According to the season, I with other boys went birdnesting, blackberrying and sometimes following the hounds. During the season, the Clifton Foot Beagles often met at the Palmer's Elm Inn and I was permitted to go with other boys and follow them all day. Clad in old clothes, we went over or through hedges and ditches and arrived home at teatime, plastered in mud. It was very exciting but my attitude now to such a sport would provide no thrills. The Clifton Foot Beagles as the name implied, were for hunting the hare on foot and no horses were permitted.

I remember on one occasion, we with other followers, were in a corner of a field, the hounds were in full cry, bearing down upon us with the frightened hare coming straight at us, until it was completely encircled into a small compass. Just as it was almost under the jaws of the leading dogs it, to my great relief, swung around and leaped right back over the pack and got away! In spite of the excitement, I am glad that I never witnessed an actual killing.

HELPING FATHER GARDENING

From about age twelve, my brother Harold had to help father in the spring digging, for which father bought an extra spade. Brother Harold also had to scrub our backyard, so when he left home to start his railway career in 1911 I had to fall in and take his place in the garden and the backyard. Scrubbing the backyard entailed dipping water from the rhine, scrubbing the bricks with a stiff broom and swilling down. I got on all right with that job until father came along and told me "to put my back into it" and also to hold the spade properly. How I wished Harold was back!

SUMMER EVENINGS AND HAROLD'S CUT HEEL

During warm summer evenings, and sometimes on a Saturday, Harold and I with other boys went bathing in the rhine. There were selected places down in the fields where the water was not out of our depth. I never became an accomplished swimmer as did Harold but we played about in the water and afterwards, as we had no towels, we ran naked around the fields to dry ourselves. A few years before, Harold used to bathe from the banks in our garden nearer the house long before I ever had a dip. Through being nearer the house there were discarded articles, such as broken china and glass and Harold cut his heel very severely. As my father picked him up to carry him indoors it was bleeding profusely and it looked as if a large part of his heel was almost severed. Even now I shudder at the memory of it. Father rendered first aid and dressed it. His heel was saved but he was crippled for quite a while as he could not wear a boot over it.

A BROKEN HANDRAIL

During one spring time I with two other boys, Stanley and Arthur Kimmins, went birdnesting. We must have been on holiday, as it was on a Friday, probably Easter. Down the lane, past the farms was a footbridge over a ditch. It was a narrow plank with a handrail and as we played around Stanley and I commenced swinging by hanging from it and of course it happened! The rail snapped and we were dropped into the water, wet up to our waists. Our stockings and trousers were saturated and we felt miserable. We tried to wring them out, and ran about to try and dry them. Then we lay in the grass hoping the sun would help. We stayed there until we thought it must be nearly tea time and then I crept home unobserved. I went into an outhouse where a heap of hay was stored for fowl's nests. I made a bed of it, covered myself with it and dropped off to sleep. Baby Ena wandering around discovered me and without waking me crept in, curled up beside me and she too dropped off to sleep. Others came looking for us to come to tea and when discovered they all came to peep at us and were highly amused. They did not wake us but allowed us to sleep on.

We were very late for tea but I did not get into trouble. The novelty of finding us asleep in the hay and the amusement it caused prevented mother from being cross but I was especially relieved that the state of my trousers escaped notice! When I got up in the morning they were still damp and looking dishevelled and mother asked me what I had done to them. I muttered something about sleeping in the hay and congratulated myself that the true cause was not revealed!

PIG KILLING AND THE SAUSAGES

When a neighbour had a pig killed it was always done in the evening and we, with other boys went to watch the butcher doing the slaughter. Then we hung around until he produced the pig's bladder which he inflated for us to use as a football, but it was shortlived and soon burst by the kicking of our heavily nailed boots. On one occasion there were two boys with us on holiday from Wolverhampton. They were what we always termed, townies, and the spectacle of a pig being slaughtered was a novelty to them. One of them caused us much amusement when he asked "And shall we see the sausages fall out?"

THE TWINS - A BIRTHDAY GRIEVANCE

It did not take us long to realise at a very early age a certain disadvantage in having to share our birthday. It is true we did not receive much but it became a grievance when we found that whereas the others might be given a shilling or sixpence, the amount was halved when our birthday came around! Nothing ever came by post and we never received birthday greetings cards - but our birthdays were always exciting. We generally had one or two friends to tea and it was part of our celebration to have a summer pudding, a dish of stewed blackberries, lined with thick slices of bread well soaked in the fruit juice.

THE VILLAGE SHOP AND BLACKSMITHS

We had only one shop in Hewish combined with the post office. It was kept by Mr H Light who was also the village blacksmith. His smithy was nearby and we often stopped to watch a horse being shod. When our iron hoops broke we took them to him to be mended. Mrs Light served in the shop and their stock consisted of a rather limited variety of essential groceries and a few jars of sweets and bags of poultry food.

We did not buy much at the shop as I mentioned before that mother had all her groceries delivered from the Co-operative at Weston. After mother had been shopping, generally in Bridgwater, she came home with a few odd farthings (¼ d) in her purse, as the price of most articles in drapers and outfitters' shops were charged to a complete number of shillings minus one farthing eg - four shillings and eleven three or nineteen and eleven three. It was considered good psychology on the part of retailers, sometimes in lieu of the farthing change to ask the customer to accept a farthing packet of pins. Mother often gave us the odd farthings with which we were able to buy a farthing's worth of sweets at the shop, as it was also the custom of other children whose pocket money was limited. But one day the shocking news went around that the shop had decided to stop selling a farthing's worth - was this the beginning of an inflationary spiral - a term which of course we did not understand. It was quite a blow and then we had to wait until we acquired a second farthing to enable us to buy a halfpennyworth.

At that time when we went into a draper's shop with mother we were fascinated by a complicated system of wires over each counter and they all led to a cashier's desk. On each wire a small round container was attached. When a purchase was completed the shop assistant placed the bill and money in the container, pulled a little handle and it was smartly catapulted along the wire to end at the cashier's desk, then quickly returned with the bill and any change due to the customer. With such a mass of wires branching out from the cashier's desk and to see the little boxes whizzing to and fro in all directions, it seemed like a toy railway!

TRAVELLING ENTERTAINERS

Occasionally travelling entertainers called at the school to ask permission of the headmaster to entertain us during the lunch hour or at playtime. My earliest recollection is of what I believe was termed a penny peepshow. We were notified the day before so that we could bring our pennies. The show consisted of a large box, brightly coloured and on two wheels like a handcart, with a pair of handles at each end. A push and pull effort for the showman and his wife. At each end of the box, low down, were two large bulls eye windows enabling four peepers to watch together. We stood side by side between the handles, our faces glued to the windows with a dark curtain pulled down over our heads and the showman operated with a system of cards from the side. By releasing a card a large picture was dropped in the centre of the box to bring it into the view of the peepers. As we watched he gave a description of the picture then raised it and dropped another. I was only about six years old and cannot remember what the pictures were, but I think they may have been replicas of well known paintings. We were only interested in the novelty of the situation and too young to understand the pictures.

PUNCH AND JUDY

A few years later we arrived at school one morning to find a Punch and Judy show set up in the playground and we were all treated to a free exhibition. It was said that the vicar, the Revd Blathwayt, had paid an overall fee to the showman for this.

I remember a rough looking gentleman of the tramp class coming into the playground to give us a show of fire eating. This was without prior notice so he was only able to collect pennies from a very few children, but everybody was able to see the performance. He lit a torch of rag, on the end of a piece of wire saturated with paraffin, and then filled his mouth from a bottle of the same and holding the lighted torch close to his mouth blew the oil over the flame, sending a stream of fire across the playground. There were murmurs of dissatisfaction from the children who had sacrificed their pennies, while the rest of us had a free show but they were mollified by the performer telling them that he would call again next week with another show - but of course he never returned!

TRAVELLING CIRCUS

One morning on our way to school we found ourselves caught up in a travelling circus, moving from Bristol to Weston and we had the excitement of walking alongside the elephants. We were told the lions were in a large horse-drawn van just ahead of us. There were also some lesser kinds of animals on foot in the procession but I forget what they were.

SHARP PRACTICE IN THE TEA TRADE

During the years prior to the First World War, although tea was sold in four ounce packets, many brands included the weight of the packing material and this consisted of a heavy leaded type of paper. Whether it contained lead, I know not, but it was of a very thick substance not unlike a very thin sheet of lead. It was also lead colour, very stiff and could be moulded into various shapes. I remember my father relating what he was told by a retail grocer. It was to the effect that when one hundredweight (112 lbs) of tea was invoiced to him, it consisted of one hundred pounds of tea and twelve pounds of the leaden packets. So when retailing his tea it consisted of about three ounces of tea and one of wrapping paper. The figures I have quoted by this example may not be the actual ones used in the trade but eventually the system was made illegal and a quarter pound of tea had to be four ounces net, that is without the wrapper, and the heavy packing material was soon replaced by ordinary light paper!

DOUBLE WEIGHT MARGARINE

About the same time a commodity appeared in the shops called "margarine". It was advertised as a substitute for butter and sold at about half the price. It was composed of vegetable oils and fats and to promote its sale and popularity a large multiple grocery firm advertised it as "double weight margarine" so that a customer purchasing one pound received two. The shop assistants could be seen feverishly weighing up one or two pound blocks. It sold like hot cakes although many housewives were hesitant about serving it up in the place of butter. It was yellow in colour and had the appearance and consistency of butter but when served as bread and butter it had a queer tang and smell when applied to the mouth. If smothered by a layer of jam though it was more palatable. Many housewives became converted to its use by using it in the mixture for cakes and pastries and by the time war broke out, in 1914, it had become well established in the butter and fat ration.

After the war, many firms packeted it and sold it under their own trade names and by this time it had become more refined and odourless but lacked the rich creamy flavour of dairy butter. Now in recent years leading dieticians proclaim the harmful effects of butter and animal fats and condemn their use for human consumption as causing heart disease, while margarine is highly commended together with vegetable cooking oils as more health giving and with less harmful results. Many margarine packets are now over printed to the effect that they are high in essential polyunsaturates and they are now more prominent on the shelves in grocers' shops and replace butter completely in many households.

THE LAST VESTIGE OF AN OLD WORLD COURTESY

During the Revd T A Robinson's incumbency at St Anne's he always went around the parish on a bicycle and this provided an opportunity for an elderly lady parishioner with her daughter on seeing him approaching, to stop and take up a position ready to drop a respectful curtsey as he passed. When however he was succeeded by the Revd Blathwayt, who travelled around on a powerful motorcycle creating a high speed, dust and noise, the good lady had to give him as wide a berth as possible, so an old world courtesy of a passing age went the way of many other picturesque customs.

HURDY GURDYS, BARREL ORGANS & ORGAN GRINDERS

There were frequently travellers on the road with a barrel organ or a Hurdy Gurdy stopping to play outside the houses and then calling at doors in the hope of a copper or two for reward. I remember a decrepit old man calling occasionally, he had a box shaped instrument slung on his back which had one leg attached on which he rested it to play by turning a handle.

SCISSOR GRINDERS

Occasionally a knife and scissor grinder passed through the village. He trundled an instrument on two wheels and when operating he was able to seat himself and work a treadle to revolve his grindstone. These hucksters also repaired umbrellas or rivetted broken china.

TRAMPS

Tramps passing through the village were frequent - they often called at doors asking for a crust of bread or a piece of left off clothing, a pair of old boots or they carried a tin can requesting a fill of hot water to make some tea and this request usually implied a spoonful of tea and sugar to go with it. We were often scared if we passed any of these rough looking customers on our way to or from school. They were usually tramping from one workhouse to another where I understand, that in return for a night's lodgings, they were given some task to perform.

Occasionally these "gentlemen of the road" were to be seen with a wire hook raking through the undergrowth along the hedges. They were searching for snails which it was understood they made a meal of but I was told they had to be roasted and I don't know how they managed that when on the road.

In later years, when in the railway service, I saw a fireman on a locomotive when the train was shunted into a sliding at a country station, occasionally searching for snails in a nearby bank. The snails were roasted by the firemen on their large coal shovels by placing them in their fire box - as they did to fry their bacon for breakfast, after hosing down the shovel when it would be as clean as a kitchen frying pan.

It was not a very frequent sight as very few in both cases seemed to aspire to the refined epicurean taste for common snails!

LOCAL CONCERTS

Mr Page, the headmaster, used to put on occasional concerts in the school room and I can just remember one in which sister Kathleen played a part as one of Bluebeards wives and the murdered wives were stood in a recess of the doorway leading to the girls cloakroom. At the back of the stage a curtain was drawn across in front of them, neck high, showing only their heads tied up by their hair to the top of the recess, giving the impression of being decapitated. I must have been about five years old because that scene is all I can recall - probably I fell asleep through most of the entertainment!

Mr Page's concerts, I believe, were to raise money to buy a huge hanging lamp for the school room. The only other lighting was by three or four lamps with reflectors but no shades fastened at intervals along the wall. They were never used during lessons on dark winter afternoons and we were never sent home early on those occasions. How different today, when I see the school room so brightly lit when passing along the road, even during the mornings.

WALKING ROUND THE WORLD

I remember when I was home from school ill during one winter, word went around that two men were passing through the village. They were walking round the world and one of them would be wearing an iron mask throughout. My mother hastily put on her hat and coat and went to the top of the lane to see them. They were selling photographs of themselves, postcard size. Mother bought one and it showed the two men pushing a perambulator, one with his head and face covered with a heavy looking mask and large placards covered the sides and front of the perambulator bearing the words "Walking round the world - the man in the iron mask!". I was very impressed at the time but I wonder now if they got any further than Bristol! Nothing more was heard of them.

CHILBLAINS

During the winter months many suffered from chilblains. We all had them on our feet and running about during playtime warmed our feet making our toes itch during lessons to a point of torture, making it difficult to concentrate on our lessons. We tried all sorts of remedies and on reaching home after school we used to toast our toes before the fire. It was said this aggravated the complaint. I have never suffered from them since leaving school at 14 years of age.

NATIONAL EVENTS DURING SCHOOL DAYS

National events which stand out in memories of my school days and which at the time, stirred the whole country were;

The death of King Edward VII in 1910,
followed by the Coronation of King George V and Queen Mary.
Captain Scott's Expedition to the South Pole - 1912-13.
The sinking of the ocean liner "Titanic" on her maiden voyage in 1912.
Outbreak of Great War - 4th August, 1914.

KING EDWARD VII's DEATH & CORONATION OF KING GEORGE V.

One fine spring morning in 1910 news came through by phone in the signal box that King Edward VII was dead. This was sensational news to us schoolchildren. I think in our childhood days there was a tendency for children to regard Kings and Queens with awe almost akin to reverence. I remember being deeply shocked when I met a boy coming across a field and I was on my way to a farm at Puxton to fetch a large jug of scalded milk, which at butter making time I think was sold for two pence. The boy was on his way back with his milk and as soon as I saw him I yelled out excitedly, "Bert, King Edward VII is dead!" I was horrified when he yelled back "Poor Old Teddy!"

The London papers went into deep mourning until the day of the funeral, all columns being divided by very thick deep black lines. There was then the excitement of the Coronation of King George V and Queen Mary which followed in 1911.

Coronation day was declared a Bank Holiday and the village celebrations took place in one of Farmer Champion's fields opposite the school. There was a meat tea provided in a large tent for the grown ups and a tea of bread and butter and cake in the school for all the children. Each child was presented with an enamelled Coronation mug, bearing a picture of King George and Queen Mary each wearing a crown.

In the afternoon, there were competitive sports for adults and children, with prizes of 1s 6d (7½ new pence). We all competed in the flat race, the obstacle race and the sack race. There were races for the grown ups too and the greatest attraction was the women's race for a greasy live pig. The poor little animal was first greased all over with vaseline or some other greasy substance, but while the men were doing the greasing, the pig escaped. When the women saw it running wildly amongst the crowd they gave chase and it was caught by a woman who fell on it and naturally claimed it. An argument ensued between the woman and a member of the committee, who insisted that the pig was not under "starter's orders", but to save an embarrassing scene over the matter, the lady was declared the winner.

SCOTT EXPEDITION TO THE SOUTH POLE - 1912

During the Spring of 1912, news of Captain Scott's Expedition to the South Pole, and his failure to make it before Amundsen, filled the national newspapers. The story of how all perished on their way back and the heroism of Captain Oates, one of the party who, when falling ill, walked out of the camp in blinding snow to die alone and avoid being a burden to his mates, and how the rest of them perished twelve days later on 29 March, made stirring reading. Our schoolmaster, Mr Farr obtained newspapers from Weston at the weekend and read the account of the shocking tragedy which stirred the nation, especially when extracts from Scott's diaries were published, which revealed the terrible hardships they suffered and the bitter disappointment of Scott at his failure to be the first to the Pole.

S S TITANIC

In the Spring of the same year, came the news of the sinking of the S S Titanic - a huge ocean liner which went down through striking an iceberg near Cape Race on her maiden voyage. The news shocked the nation as the ship was said to be unsinkable. Hundreds of lives were lost owing to there being insufficient lifeboats to take the passengers and crew. At that period, there was an emigration boom and hundreds of men were going out to Canada and Australia in the hopes of making their fortunes and with better prospects than were available in the home country.

In our village the tragedy of the Titanic was brought home to us more sensationally, on account of the fact that a man from Hewish was a passenger who went down with the ship. He was John Gill, who was a chauffeur to our vicar, the Revd Blathwayt.

SINKING OF THE S S TITANIC - APRIL 1912.

Copy of hymn composed by the Revd Blathwayt,
Vicar of St Anne's, Hewish.

Sung at the Memorial Service in the church
on the Sunday following receipt of the news.

REV. xxi 1-4

1.
For those afar from Home,
Not knowing what betide
What happiness or gloom
The evening shadows hide
Pray when sweet echoes round thee throng
Of bells that chime for Evensong.

2.
The hush of eventide
The ocean calm and clear
The tireless engine's glide
Bespeak no peril near
Yet silently across the main
There floats the dreaded Arctic plain.

3.
The twilight fades; good night
Sleep closes tired eyes,
Astern the track gleams white,
Ahead black peril lies
Between the maindeck and the keel
The icy share hath ploughed like steel.

4.
Gored by the unseen floe;
The dreaded waves conceal
The riven plates below,
Through which death's waters steal,
Pray thou; yet learn that God is nigh.
To human souls in agony.

5.
Pray thou, and still thy grief.
The angels while we kneel
Bring some the near relief
To some the heavens reveal
Who will deny that they are blest
To whom God's answer bringeth rest.

6.
Nearer, O God, to thee
The souls in wonder climb
From out the shrouding sea
To greet the Light Sublime
Lord Jesus bless us as we kneel
And let thy pardoning mercy heal

AMEN

C R B - St Anne's, Hewish   *April, 1912.*

The offertories were given to the widowed bride of the late John Gill
whose wife was a domestic servant in the vicarage. It was Mr Gill's
intention, as it was with many others at that time, to go out first and as
soon as they were established in suitable work, for their wives to follow
them.

The Gill's were a newly married couple when they entered the vicar's service and this to local minds seemed to intensify the sense of tragedy. On the Sunday following receipt of the news, the Revd Blathwayt arranged a Memorial Service in the evening for which he composed the above special hymn which was sung to the tune of a well-known children's hymn in the Ancient and Modern Hymn book - "Hushed was the evening hymn". Mr Farr (our headmaster) as was usual obtained some London newspapers at the weekend and read us the account of the tragedy in which items of heroism by individual passengers were recounted in glowing terms. Especially the fact that as the ship was struck the ship's band was playing the hymn "Nearer my God to Thee", it being a Sunday evening and at our Memorial Service the hymn was included. Ever since, whenever that hymn is sung at a church service, the loss of the Titanic comes to mind in those who can recall the tragedy.

During the emigration boom referred to, the Governments of Canada and Australia were offering tempting inducements to young men from the mother country to emigrate and I believe free or assisted passages and prospects of acquiring large tracts of land were among the facilities offered. To young labouring men in our rural villages, with no prospects of advancement, these inducements proved very attractive.

Two lads from Puxton, brothers by the name of Palmer and a cousin of the same name, decided to embark on the great adventure to Australia. It was indeed considered a great adventure - sensational in fact, when it meant a six weeks sea voyage with no news of their arrival for another six weeks! So a few days prior to their departure the Revd Blathwayt arranged a well attended farewell service one evening in our church and during the period of their voyage prayers were offered at our church services for their safe arrival and the hymn "For those in Peril on the Sea" was frequently sung.

A few years later after the outbreak of war in 1914, the brothers volunteered for service in France and this enabled them to visit England when on leave.

Now in Puxton church is erected a white marble tablet commemorating one of the brothers, W Palmer of an Australian regiment, killed in action during the Battle of the Somme in 1916.

OUTBREAK OF THE FIRST WORLD WAR

The outbreak of war on 4 August, 1914 was greeted in a far different manner from that of the second world war in 1939. A wave of patriotic hysteria swept the whole country and a strong recruiting drive affected every village and hamlet. Large recruiting posters appeared on every hoarding and young men in every village rushed to volunteer to join the services. One man, Richard Kimmins, who was a reservist and worked on the railway, was immediately called up and eventually killed in France.

I remember a huge poster of Lord Kitchener appeared. It depicted him pointing a finger at you and it said "Your King and Country need you!". We were greatly impressed by this picture as the finger seemed to point at one from whatever angle it was viewed. The poster became famous and it has often since been reprinted, I suppose on account of its artistic merit.

Both the Revd Blathwayt and our school master, Mr F G Farr, were enthusiastic patriots. The former addressed recruiting meetings around the district in which he read a patriotic poem entitled "The Day" written by H Chappell, a railwayman in Bath. Then he announced that he would convey the first man in our village who volunteered, in his car to the centre where he had to report on being called up. The first man was a farm labourer who worked for Farmer Jones, but was not a local and was unknown to us. On the appointed day, he was picked up at the vicarage just after we had assembled for morning school and we all had to stand out in the road to cheer as the car came out of the vicarage drive, to proceed to Bristol accompanied by the vicar and driven by his chauffeur. The car was an open Ford and as we cheered lustily and waved vigorously the hero leaned out over the back of the car waving his hat furiously as the car disappeared in a cloud of dust.

There was a brisk sale of miniature Union Jacks made of cotton and more expensive ones of silk. Many cyclists had one screwed into their front mudguard. Thousands of recruits were billeted in private houses in Weston super Mare and for a while had to train and drill in civvy clothes until the factories produced sufficient khaki uniforms and heavy army boots. Within a few weeks, long processions of these recruits passed through the village on route marches. Sometimes they were headed by a military band with the men singing the latest pantomime songs, but always one heard, "It's a long way to Tipperary" as this song achieved fame through newspapers and reports that the first contingents of our men on landing in France sung it as they marched up to the front line trenches.

These route marches were almost a daily occurrence. When without a band, the men whistled popular tunes and with a procession of several hundreds stretching over half a mile, their whistling could be heard long before they came into sight and also after they had passed. There were of course many tenderfoots among them, men who were not used to wearing such heavy boots as those supplied by the army, neither were some of them used to walking any distances and they certainly did not whistle and were obviously relieved when an accompanying army vehicle picked them up. These troops were embarrassing to any school girl who happened to be passing them when alone, as they were greeted with wolf whistles and light frivolities as they passed - but when in the company of other girls, I think they enjoyed it!

BOY SCOUTS

To encourage recruiting among local men in the Weston area a separate company was formed called the Old Comrades Battalion and just before Christmas a big display of their drilling and training was organised on the Beach Lawns at Weston with accompanying bands. This is where the Boy Scouts also came to the fore. Soon after the war broke out Mr Farr organised a troop in our village (more about that later). Our troop consisted of two patrols and we were called upon with all the scouts in the district, to assemble and encircle the Beach Lawns to keep the crowd back which we did by using our scout staves - five feet long stout ashpoles which were part of scouts' traditional equipment then, but now dispensed with. Each scout grasped the end of his stave on one side and the end of his neighbour's on the other side. Thus the scouts were spaced five feet apart all around the lawns and provided an effective fence to keep the lawns clear for the comrades to carry out their drilling display. Hundreds of the townsfolk came to watch their local comrades. My mother and sisters, of course, came to watch and I remember one of my sisters creeping through the crowd behind me and pressing a toffee into my hand! It was a proud moment for us scouts when patriotic fervour was at its height.

1915.

The route marches of all these recruits came to an end in the early Spring when they were drafted elsewhere or overseas to complete their training. When later the casualty lists of killed, wounded or missing in France, were listed in the daily papers the hysterical patriotic fervour which greeted the outbreak of war took a more sober tune. When the first few local men from the Weston district were brought home wounded, the local papers contained long accounts with interviews stressing their cheerfulness and how they said they could not get well quickly enough to return to France to have another crack at the Huns. The mood changed though when the casualty lists included local men killed in action. One victim was a Hewish lad, well known to us all - Reg Neath, and as he was a school boy of about 20 years of age it brought the seriousness of war right home to us.

On Sundays at church the vicar regularly read out the Roll of Honour of all Hewish and Puxton men who were serving with the forces. A few weeks later this included our schoolmaster Mr Frank Farr, but he returned safely after serving in Salonica and becoming Staff Sergeant Major. Then the vicar announced that at 12 noon the church bell should be rung to remind people to offer prayers for the safe return of our men. He came into the school and asked Mr Farr to allow a boy to leave school five minutes before twelve each day to go to the tower and ring the bell for five minutes. As I was then the senior boy, it fell to me to carry out this duty. It was stressed what a great honour this was to be assigned the duty and the vicar said he would duly reward me with some sort of presentation, but although I regularly rang the bell until I left home in April 1915 to start my career on the railway, the Revd Blathwayt's memory failed him and a present never materialised.

HORSES COMMANDEERED

Another memory which impressed us school boys was when an official came around and commandeered suitable horses from the farmers for war purposes. The Army was far from being mechanised and as most boys knew the names of many of the farmers' horses it was sensational. I remember a fine chestnut horse owned by our neighbour, Mr Williams was taken - its name was Marquis.

BOY SCOUTS - FORMATION OF HEWISH TROOP

During the Summer of 1914 one of my father's colleagues from Yatton gave me Baden Powell's book, "Scouting for Boys". It belonged to his son now grown up and I was thrilled with it. Baden Powell immediately became my hero! I later took the book to school to lend to a school mate and as I passed it to him under the desk during lessons it caught the eye of Mr Farr and he immediately demanded to see it. He glanced through it and became interested, so instead of a reprimand it was, "This is interesting, I would like to borrow it". Then when war broke out he was fired with the idea of forming a troop of boy scouts and of course several boys were thrilled at the prospect.

Next there followed a visit from the County Commissioner, Mr G E Wollen, a headmaster of Etonhurst Private School for Boys in Weston. He came into school and addressed us on the aims and principles of the scout movement. He came wearing the scout uniform of that period and from then on a dozen boys were full of enthusiasm. Two patrols of six boys were formed, the Fox and Wolf patrols. I was appointed Patrol Leader of the former. Mr Farr became our Scout Master. Then the question of uniform arose and it was obvious hardly any of the boys could afford a complete outfit so we had to acquire it bit by bit. To commence, Mr Farr ordered our stout ashen staves, 5ft long and markings in feet lengths burnt into them. They are obsolete now, but it was an essential item of equipment then. I think they cost 1s 6d (7½ pence). Next we obtained felt hats and khaki shirts and I believe the shirts were 3s 6d (17½ pence) and hats about 3s (15 pence). Later we bought our billy cans, haversacks and belts and this completed our issue.

We never acquired khaki shorts to complete the official outfit so boys had to wear their everyday trousers which were then worn with stockings and the legs were fastened by a buckle just below the knee. But my mother made me a pair of navy blue shorts from a pair of my father's discarded uniform and I was a very proud chap indeed.

As Patrol Leader I was provided with a whistle attached to a white lanyard. I also carried our patrol flag on route marches - a triangular shape of cotton material on which was imprinted a brightly coloured brown fox which I attached to my stave with tapes at the corners. Mr Farr accompanied us on Saturday afternoons on our route marches during the Autumn. We walked across the fields to join the river Yeo which we followed down to Woodspring where we crossed to Sand Bay and there we had our tea by brewing up on a fire over which we made a tripod of three staves on which we hung our billy cans to boil. It was great fun! We also marched to Sandford Hill and on that occasion were joined by members of the Worle troop. We had our tea in a copse up on the hill but that portion of the hill has disappeared by quarrying.

We were fortunate too in being allocated a scout room situated in the old Post Office yard with access by a flight of steps. It was furnished with chairs including two large Berkeley type and a large basket work easy chair. It also had a fire grate and a quarter size billiard table. The room had previously been the Working Mans Club instituted by the Revd Blathwayt but it gradually faded out through lack of support.

We were able to attend every evening and we made good use of it. We took firewood for the fire grate and made good use of the billiard table too. There being no chalk available to use on the cues it became the habit to point our cues to the ceiling and rub them in the limewash. Eventually the ceiling was covered with cue marks and some even went right through the plaster! Oh, they were great times and happy days.

Then one afternoon I had a thrilling surprise, the Revd Blathwayt came into school and presented me with my second class badge. This was quite unexpected, as I had not taken any test to win it but I think it was Mr Farr's doing and it was by way of encouragement. I was a very keen and dedicated scout and no doubt the confiscation of my Scouting for Boys book, which I have already mentioned, was the means of our Scout Troop being formed.

SCOUT KNIVES

The regulation scout knife was a large one, bladed with a marline spike - a fairly thick pointed spike which opened and closed like the blade on the opposite side. It was provided as a tool for splicing ropes. It was one of the first requirements of a Scout to learn to tie various knots. A few of the boys bought real scout knives and on the blade was engraved "Boy Scout". It had a metal link to attach it to the scout belt. I could not muster the one shilling and sixpence or maybe two shillings.

But in November, 1914, my grandmother Westcott had died in Exeter, where she lived in a couple of rooms in Springfield Road, and it fell to me to go down to Exeter for a few days to assist my Aunt Emily (father's only sister) to clear up grandma's belongings before vacating the rooms. I happened to possess one shilling and I saw some large pocket knives in a shop window at 10½ d (about 3½ new pence). I immediately purchased one - it was a type very common then, with two blades side by side, a large one and a smaller one. Folded over on the other side was a little metal hook said to be used for extracting stones jammed in horses hooves, and inserted in grooves cut down through the bone handle were a toothpick and a small pair of tweezers. I came home and was very pleased to display my new knife and one scout, Lewis Edwards, (nicknamed Brownie because he always wore a dark brown corduroy suit, knickerbockers and a Norfolk jacket) was very taken with my new possession and he offered to exchange it for his real scout knife. I immediately agreed as I was more proud to own the real article! Poor Brownie was about one year older than I and he was later killed on active service in France. The knife is still in my possession.

SCHOOL - SUMMER HOLIDAYS AT EXETER

During our Summer holidays in the years around 1905-12 the whole family went to stay at grandma Westcott's at Exeter for about 2 weeks. At that time my father was allowed only three days annual leave but mother stayed on longer with us.

I remember her making preparations for several days beforehand, washing and ironing my sisters' best dresses and packing them in a large telescopic wicker basket which was secured by a leather strap. Then on the day of departure we went to Puxton station in a neighbours' high pony-cart (father came on later when he had finished duty - he walked down the line and caught a later train from Puxton). At that time there was always the risk of his leave being cancelled at very short notice if no relief was available so he lost no time in getting away before he could be recalled! Then on arrival at Exeter mother ordered a horse and cab from the cabstand to take us up to Springfield Road - this was exciting for us children!

When at Exeter we always made a pilgrimage to the village of Ide (pronounced Ede) my father's birthplace and where his father was buried. He died at the early age of 28 when my father was about five years old. When we visited grandpa's grave, as it was usually on a Sunday, we went to the Evening Service at the church. Grandma was proud to tell us that grandpa Westcott was one of the bellringers to ring the first peal after the church was rebuilt and the bells re-hung, that was shortly before he died.

Whilst at Exeter, on one or two occasions we went to Bridford to visit my father's uncle Jeremiah at Burnicombe Farm. We went by train to Christow. It was quite a long way to the farm and uncle met us with horse and wagon. It was a rough narrow road and the farm was down in a steep hollow. It was very isolated and the village was further down a steep path through a wood. Burnicombe was a small farmstead and uncle kept two or three cows and two heavy carthorses named Brandy and Dumpling. Aunt Mary Ann baked her own bread and made her own butter. I have a vague memory of being there on an earlier occasion when about five years of age and wandering downstairs very early when uncle and aunt were up and about. Aunt Mary Ann sat me on a stool in the great open hearth where a big wood fire was blazing and gave me a good slice of bread with a thick coating of cream atop!

HAROLD AND THE BEES!

I can just remember too that in the garden beneath the kitchen window uncle had three or four hives of bees. They were in the old style straw skips on wooden stands. That was at the time, I believe, when to take the honey the bees had to be destroyed over a sulphur pit. Brother Harold was curious enough to poke a stick in the entrance of one of the hives with the result that he was badly stung. I remember the commotion it caused and the "blue-bag" was much in evidence.

LATER YEARS AT GRANDMA'S

When we were a little older we went away on our own. I went to stay with grandma Westcott at Exeter. Grandma Westcott was regarded as the boy's grandma while grandma Scaly at Bridgwater as the girl's grandma and my sisters Kathleen and Gertrude went there to stay. There were three girl cousins living next door and so my sisters had pleasant company there. The cousins then had their holidays later in August (ours were in June-July) and then they came to stay with us at Hewish and we had a lovely time scrumping apples in the orchard down our lane, the owner of which lived three or four miles away. Brother Harold went to stay at Burnicombe in Bridford.

I was a great favourite of grandma Westcott's and I am afraid she spoilt me. She first lived in Springfield Road and later in Hoopern Street. There were plenty of boys around with whom I could play and I got to know several. A cousin of my father's also lived at Exeter and kept a large boarding house at No 6 Northernhay Place and a boy from

Swindon stayed there for his holiday at about the same time. I spent a lot of time with him and we used to walk down to the River Exe with nets and jam jars catching minnows.

Occasionally on fine afternoons grandma dressed up in her fineries and her smart bonnet and carrying a sunshade walked in the Park, Northernhay or Bury Meadow, or maybe went out for some special shopping. I remember her saying she wanted some stronger spectacles so we went down to the market where there was a stall with a loose pile of spectacles in steel frames. Would-be customers sorted them over and tried them on - testing them by reading a printed card on display. When grandma found a pair which she decided was an improvement on her old ones, she bought them for one shilling.

When staying with her we always walked out to Ide on a Sunday evening if fine, to attend the service at church and to look at grandpa Westcott's grave. It was quite a long walk from Hoopern Street, down through the town to St Thomas's and then across the fields.

On one occasion Harold was also there and one fine afternoon we walked out to Ide with grandma where she decided to call on an old friend, a very old lady named Mrs Cann who lived in a tiny cottage and was obviously very poor. The door opened straight into her living room and it looked very poverty stricken. We were not permitted to enter but grandma sat just inside and was given a cup of tea. Then the old lady gave us one to share in a huge enamelled mug, I believe because no other cups were available, and we had to drink it sitting on a stone on the garden path. But this huge old mug tickled us immensely and as I put it to my lips Harold started to shake with laughter which of course was infectious and I could not drink. The same thing happened when Harold tried to drink and we both laughed uproariously - so much of the tea was spilt. I hesitate to estimate the capacity of that old mug for fear of exaggeration, but I have never been offered a cup of tea that size since! Then of course grandma, observing us from the doorway, gave her tongue free play about our bad manners but Brother Harold and I often laughed heartily over it during the years when we recalled our visit to Old Mother Cann's at Ide!

Grandma's house in Hoopern Street was next to the wall of the Army Barracks. It was very high and I could not see over it, except in the attic bedroom where I slept and in the early morning I used to climb up and kneel on the dressing table to watch the soldiers drilling. This was always before grandma brought me up an early morning cup of tea and a biscuit when she used to sit and chatter for a while.

One morning, as she sat beside the dressing table she started fingering the various articles among which was a hand mirror with a wooden back. It was lying face downwards and as she picked it up the glass was left on the table lying in splinters but still in its perfect shape. As the table was higher than my bed I could not see this but I did see the astounded look on her face! She then looked at me with the same queer look, and with the wooden mirror back, raising it like a tennis racket, she gave me some hand slaps the cause for which I was entirely ignorant, but later I knew how it happened. I, when watching the soldiers knelt on the mirror and broke the glass into a fine array of splinters. Poor grandma then realised too how it happened, she was very upset and never ceased to regret how she slapped the poor little chap!

MY FIRST ENCOUNTER WITH THE LAW!

When about seven years of age, on a fine summer afternoon, for some unknown reason I arrived home after the others, and as I dawdled down our lane I saw mother sat out on the bridge. She had cleaned up early and was doing some needlework. On the opposite side stood the policeman under the signal box. It was either PC Greed or PC Standen from Congresbury and it was one of their scheduled meeting points. I could not see him until I arrived beside mother who must have spoken about my dawdling. When I saw the policeman, he said something to the effect that if I did not come home earlier he would put me in his lock-up! My word! Wasn't I frightened! I went and sat up close to mother trembling violently and how my knees knocked together. Although many parents often threatened their children by telling the policeman when they misbehaved, this was the only occasion mother did it and how she regretted it when she saw my frightened state!

HEWISH HARVEST HOME

Many Somerset villages were noted for their Harvest Homes and ours was generally regarded as an outstanding celebration. In those days it was essentially a village affair, and was patronised only by a few from neighbouring parishes who came by pony trap. It was a day of merry making combined with the harvest thanksgiving service in the church. A large marquee was erected in the field near the church and following the service which was held in the morning the celebrations commenced. There were sports and races for grown ups and children and a high tea for the grown ups. The farmers wives provided huge joints of ham and beef and the meal was served rather late to enable the farm workers to share in it after milking time. A brass band was hired for dancing in the evening and it went on until midnight. Everything was free to the parishioners, including a tea for all the schoolchildren and for this we always had to take our own mugs. The marquee was illuminated by oil flares in the early days. It was always held on a Friday with following up services in the church on Sunday. Harvest Homes were an institution celebrated from very early times and I believe Hewish commenced theirs with the building of the church, vicarage and school in 1865, but it may have commenced before that.

I remember how the older folks recalled the occasion when a gale blew the marquee down but that happened before my time. The church was always decorated with flowers and every window shelf was loaded with various fruits and vegetables, also there was a display around the font and on the chancel steps. What a delightful aroma it provided the mixture of apples, flowers and vegetables gave off a pleasant peculiar scent which pervaded every church during Harvest Thanksgiving and I remember giant marrows were much in evidence. My father always gave a huge basket of his potatoes specially selected from his crop. On the following Monday a farmer loaded up his horse and cart and took all the fruit and veg to Weston Hospital. At that time the gifts were most welcome as the hospitals relied on voluntary contributions only, with no financing by the state.

The chapel also had their thanksgiving service but they always auctioned their produce on the following Monday, preceded by an extra thanksgiving service and the proceeds went into their own local funds towards their expenses. This was the common practice in all country nonconformist churches.

Now everything has changed, both the Harvest Homes and the thanksgivings. The Harvest Home at Hewish is no longer essentially a village affair. Indeed many local residents do not partake. It is run on highly commercial lines and it is attended by hundreds who come from near and far. The field with the marquee is now a huge fun fair with roundabouts and other mechanical amusements all costing money. A high class lunch is served and the costly tickets are sold in advance. The offerings of fruit and vegetable in the church are no longer made from the villagers own gardens and this for two reasons. Firstly, many of them do not cultivate a large vegetable garden so necessary in bygone days to maintain the family throughout the year, and secondly, the hospitals do not now rely on the huge gifts of local produce which came in from all the villages around.

I miss that delightful aroma so characteristic of every church at the thanksgiving service and which is never experienced elsewhere, not even in a greengrocer's shop. Nowadays if there are any offerings displayed in the church they consist of tins of preserved foods, eg meats, soups, fruits, fish etc. and usually held to give out by sick visitors in the parishes during the winter.

THE FIRST "FLYING MACHINE"

In 1912 or 1913 (I think it was the latter) flying machines became a talking point when I was on holiday at Exeter staying with grandma Westcott. The subject gained prominence at that time as one of the London daily papers was offering a prize of a few thousand pounds for the fastest flier from London to the West of England and it was said that a stop would be made at Exeter. The competitors would fly on different days and the first competitor was expected on a day while I was at grandma's, but no information was available as to where it would land. Grandma was most anxious that I should see my first flying machine and from talking with various folks it was generally thought that the landing would be in a field well outside the city but near the railway, as following the railway line would be the best navigational aid available. Someone mentioned to grandma that it might be near Lion Halt, a small country station on the London and South Western.

So grandma decided that we should make our way there by going in to Exeter and then finding our way well out into the country where we wandered around the fields expecting to see a landing at any moment. I had visions of crowds of people roaming the fields for the same purpose, but wandering from field to field for many hours we were completely alone with only cattle grazing for company. After walking around for several hours we gave up and went home, tired and very disappointed. Then a day or two later one actually arrived and landed somewhere near the city and the Exeter Hippodrome advertised that it would be shown on the cinema screen the following evening. So grandma, to make up for my disappointment gave me a few coppers to go with another boy to see it. Just before it was due to appear on the screen, the manager announced very apologetically that for some technical reasons the film was not a success and all we saw was a hazy figure of a man in what seemed a thick fog spinning a propeller. The failure was obviously poor photography as no flier at that time would take off in anything but clear weather and presumably cinephotography was not sufficiently advanced to make reliable clear reproductions outside the studio.

At that time the term aeroplane had not become the more sophisticated term for flying machines just as cinematographs were referred to as living pictures and later talking pictures. Similarly gramophones were referred to as talking machines among village folk.

However, after returning home and commencing school after the holidays, another plane passed over Hewish one fine morning just before leaving for school. Word came via the signal box telephone that one was on its way following the railway line. Within a short while after receiving the message it came into view and what excitement! It was really a nine days wonder and compared with the giants of today, carrying three or four hundred passengers, it looked a very flimsy affair indeed with the pilot exposed and plainly seen. It was a talking point with both children and grown ups for several days. I did not see another until 1917 when I was moved to Coalpit Heath near Filton after my first two and half years on the railway at Wookey. By that time rapid advances in aeronautics had been made, no doubt in feverish haste for use on the battle fronts, and Filton became a busy centre for building planes and training pilots so in that area they had become a common everyday sight.

MY FIRST RIDE IN A MOTOR CAR

Strange to relate I had not at that time ridden in a motor car and that wonderful experience did not come my way until the summer of 1914. Very few cars passed through the village, they had not replaced the horse and cart except that charabancs (charrybangs!!) were becoming popular for day trippers from Bristol to Weston mainly at weekends, gradually ousting the wagonette and the four-horse brake. Many people were nervous of the new form of travel with the higher speed and dust they produced on our limestone roads as yet untarred.

Now my first car ride happened like this! One fine hot summer afternoon on a Saturday, my father, when setting out on his bicycle to commence duty at 2 pm at Puxton station, had a puncture. So he took mother's cycle and left instructions for me to follow later and wheel his cycle to the signal box where he would have time to effect a repair while I rode back home on mother's cycle. The distance was about 2 miles and it was a very hot and dusty walk which I did not relish. I had not gone far when I heard a car approaching and I knew that as it passed I would be covered in dust, so feeling contrary I said to myself as I loitered in the middle of the road, "I'll make him sound his horn before I move out of its way". Then to my consternation he drew up and stopped beside me. Now I thought "I m in for a wigging" but to my surprise he shouted, "Going very far son?" Upon telling him my destination he said, "Perhaps I can give you a lift?" Now it happened to be a sports car and I recognised its number too, through seeing it so often. It was "BO 80" and I recalled that in pronouncing it, it spelt "BOAT". It was a very low two seater and had a folding hood which when not in use lay well back on the rear of the car. He took the cycle and laid it across the hood telling me to hold on to it and keep it in position as I sat sideways. So I arrived at Puxton in fine style. This experience then was to me almost as great a thrill as the sight of the first aeroplane already mentioned.

OAK APPLE DAY

On the 29 May during my first few years at school the children celebrated Oak Apple Day in a most weird fashion. Some of the bigger boys and girls chased the others with a bunch of stinging nettles and one was only exempt from being stung by wearing an oak apple but as there were no oak apple trees in our area, a spray of maple leaves was accepted as a substitute. As one was being chased the assailant when brandishing the nettles, shouted the following ditty;

"It's the 29 May - Oak Apple Day

If you don't give us a holiday - we'll run away"

The whole game seemed pointless as the ditty could only apply to the school master (but he was never attacked!). It was rather frightening to us younger children and the custom faded out, but I don't know how or when it was introduced and I wonder if it was observed by any other school round about. There was never any reference to Charles II and I wonder if those wielding the nettles were aware of the historic connection!

HAYMAKING

During 1912,13 and 14 I spent most of my summer holiday haymaking on our neighbour's farm. We always had five weeks holiday during June and July and either the first two or the last two weeks were spent at Exeter, but in 1914 I preferred to stay at home and spend the whole of my holiday haymaking.

As the men could not go to the hayfield until milking was completed we did not commence until we had our breakfast at home, except for one boy who accompanied George Watts at 5 am when he started mowing and one boy was required to rake back behind the machine. There were usually two other boys of my age taken on for the season and I enjoyed it immensely. Haymaking was not such a mechanised process as it is now and all the operations in the field were by horse power. Our duties were often very hard work but it was fun. The mechanical aids in the hayfield were firstly the mowing machine drawn by two heavy cart-horses, then a swathe-turner for the first turning of the rows after mowing and the upper side of each row had dried but the underside was green and damp. Next would come a tedder drawn by one horse for tossing the hay to hasten drying, then the horse-rake, used to rake the hay into wakes by drawing it up into long rows for collecting by a horse-drawn collector, a sledge like implement with long teeth on lines which skimmed along the ground gathering up the long rows and drawing it into the hayricks.

Hayricks were made in every field away from the farm where they could be used to feed the stock grazing there in the winter. Two boys were positioned on a rick being built, to take the hay from the men (usually two) pitching it up from the ground and with their hay forks (or peaks as we called them) we boys passed it back to the farmer who spread it around evenly and kept the rick in shape, usually round, square or oblong. It was quite a skilled job to keep the rick from being one-sided as it grew higher and Mr Jones always did that job himself. Other jobs for the boys were raking the mown grass from the edges of the field where it could be more accessible for the swathe turner, horse rake or tedder, and when rain was threatened, and the hay was dry, we had to assist the men in making it into haycocks. These were shapely heaps three to four feet high and the farmer was insistent that we topped each cock with wisps of hay lying evenly in one direction in a form of impromptu thatch to cause the water to drain off rather than soak into the hay beneath.

Farmer Jones's wife was noted for feeding the men well (meals were provided for the men only during harvest time) when in fields away from the farm. The grub was brought out to us by the farmer's son in the horse and float (a light two wheeled cart used for taking the churns of milk to the railway station as at that time all milk was sent by rail). At eleven o'clock we all gathered round under the rick and farmer cut out huge chunks of bread and cheese and passed them around with the gallon cider jar. Mrs Jones sent out a jar of cocoa or lemonade for the boys and we made short work of that!

Daily during hay making the butcher's boy cycled down from Congresbury with a huge joint of beef and at dinner time a good roast meal of new potatoes, green peas and carrots was served out in the same manner as the bread and cheese lunch, brought out with the necessary plates and cutlery. After eating, the men had a short nap but we boys fooled around and sometimes surrepticiously grabbed a jar of cider and had a good swig. Farmer Jones worked in conjunction with his son's farm, Palmer's Elm, situated about a mile away down the road to Wick St Lawrence and the men from both farms combined forces for the haymaking so that working in the field were Farmer Jones, his two sons, four labourers, we boys and an extra man taken on just for the haymaking. Also in the evening my father or Mr Bailey came along occasionally to help us for an hour or two. We worked until nearly dusk and then all went into the farmhouse for a good supper of ham and cheese. Mrs Jones was a typical storybook type of farmer's wife. A motherly soul, short and rotund and with her two daughters worked very hard all day cooking and catering for such a number of men who all ate heartily through toiling and sweating all day in the hayfields. Those meals are still a happy memory.

When we finished at one farm we all went to work at the other. Farmer Jones was very progressive, he was the only one who had a hay loading elevator driven by a stationary petrol engine and at the Palmer's Elm farm he had a windmill in the yard to pump drinking water into tanks around the farm for the animals. The elevator was used to fill the two big hay barns. It was hoisted above the roof from which a sheet of galvanised iron was removed for the hay to be dropped down inside and two boys stood ready to take it and pass it back to the farmer. The men feeding the elevator from a wagon load were able to push huge quantities over and we boys were almost buried but we had to be quick to pass it back before another huge quantity was dropped on us.

There were then two fields at Dolmoor about half way to Congresbury where we turned into a long lane by a shed always known as the Oxhouse (it is still there). One summer I was given the job of going up to these fields with George Watts who always drove the mowing machine at 5 am in the morning to do the raking back.

Mowing was always done very early in the morning and when at Dolmoor Mr Jones's son brought us out breakfast of fried bacon and eggs at about 9 o'clock after the milking was done at the farm. It was a very long day as we did not leave the field until about 9 pm and although it was such a long day, how I enjoyed it! At the end of the day the machines were left in the fields until all was gathered in. Then the men were driven home to the farm but the two carthorses had to be ridden home to stable and that is where we boys came in. We quarrelled about who was to ride them home (3 boys to 2 horses). They were lovely animals named Violet and Darling, the former was the daughter of the latter and she had a colt left at home in the stable and how she galloped all the way. There was no holding her back and we rode bare back - Oh! it was great fun.

That year my mother arranged to go down to Devonshire with my sisters and I was to take a trip on the river to Dartmouth, but I refused to go, preferring to stay at home to go haymaking.

The fields at Dolmoor were the last fields to be harvested and on clearing up Mr Jones on the way home drove into the Full Quart Inn and treated us to drinks all round and we boys had our fill of lemonade or ginger beer.

RICKS AND THATCHERS

In those days the whole of the hay was made into ricks or stored in haybarns erected in the farmyard. The system of baling under pressure with a bailing machine did not become practice until years later. Ricks were always made in the outlying fields so that the hay was immediately available to be cut in trusses and given to the cattle when grazing there. For this a murderous looking knife was used to cut out the trusses.

It was a large triangular piece of steel with the cutting edge on the curved side of the blade. The system of ricks called for the thatchers' skills as soon as the rick was built and settled. Not all farmers or their men could thatch a rick, but there were men around who were qualified thatchers and in great demand at the end of haymaking. Nowadays the sight of a thatched hayrick in a field is a rarity. With modern tractors and trailers hay can be easily cut out from the hay barn and transported to the field.

A HAY KNIFE

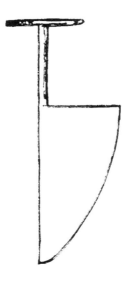

As I have mentioned elsewhere my father was taught the art of thatching in his boyhood days when living on a farm with his uncle but gave it up after a few years to enter the railway service. When living at Hewish it gave him great pleasure, when asked, to thatch a little rick for his neighbour, Mr John Ball, who saved the hay made in his orchard to feed his pony during the winter. My father also enjoyed cutting and splitting willows to make the spars necessary for pegging down the thatches. Now several years later the system of baling has come into use and the hay knife dispensed with. The hay is stacked in pressed bales weighing about a half hundredweight and can be easily handled and distributed around the field.

WAGES

We were not paid a fixed wage and did not expect one but some time after haymaking when meeting Farmer Jones on the road he stopped and gave me about three shillings and sixpence (17½ pence) and I was very well satisfied. That amount incidentally was my brother Harold's weekly wage when he was taken on at the farm for a few weeks on leaving school at age 14 in April, 1911. This job was to fill the waiting period until he joined the railway as a Lad Porter. Harold had to start early to milk the cows. Milking machines were only just becoming popular so all the farmers still milked by hand. His meals were provided at the farm so it meant that mother had one mouth less to feed which no doubt was a consideration when we were all very hearty eaters!

It is interesting to recall that farmers at that time were no better educated than their employees but they were conscious of their superiority by virtue of their economic position. Consequently they developed an attitude of snobbishness, and as a class, developed a social life in the village (dances, whist drives, etc.) exclusively for themselves. This attitude was apparent among the farmer's children even at school. There being no gentry resident in the village they were big fishes in a very little pond and the labouring population were mainly employees of the farmers. But our family and that of Mr Bailey (father's opposite number previously mentioned) were in a class of our own consequently it was not necessary for us to adopt an attitude of subservience as did many of the labourers' children. This was particularly noticeable when we were working at haymaking time when the labourers boys were expected to refer to the farmers' children as Miss G or Master H, although they were schoolmates and sat together in class. I refrained from this attitude of servility and apparently my snobbish superiority over the labourers' boys was recognised and accepted. Apart from this form of shallow thinking most of the farming families were very decent and kindly folk. (The Master H and Miss G of course was not observed in the school playground).

CIDER MAKING

In the Autumn was the apple harveSt. Every farm had an apple orchard generally near the farmhouse and the apples were grown solely for cider making. Large quantities were always made as it was an all-year-round drink for the farmers' families and also to provide a daily allowance for the workers and consumption in the haymaking season was very heavy. When out in the hayfield and the gallon earthenware jars needed replenishing it fell to one of the boys to go back to the house for refills. No mugs were provided, everyone drank straight from the jar.

Many farms had a cider press which was worked by a horse harnessed to a long beam fixed in the open yard near the cider house and by a system of cogs the horse walked around in a circle which transmitted power by a revolving bar and operated the crusher. When the apples were reduced to a pulp they were placed in a large press in layers between hair cloths and the juiced squeezed out into a tank. Even some cottages had a cider orchard and they took their apples to a neighbouring farm to provide them with a supply of cider to last through the year.

The apples were rarely of a decent quality but we children knew where one or two choice varieties existed when we were scrumping. In Gill's orchard down our lane there was a tree of Blenheims and Russetts and of course plenty of Morgan Sweets as these were popular for cider making. The end product varied in quality from farm to farm, it varied little from season to season and on account of the types of apples grown it could be recognised and everyone agreed that Farmer So & So's cider was pretty poor stuff!

I remember Farmer Chapman at Pool Farm was noted for his high quality cider, for which he gained prizes at the shows. It was said he produced such good stuff, on account of his orchard being composed mainly of Kingston Blacks, reputed to be a first class cider apple. During cider making time the strong scent of crushed and fermenting apples pervaded the atmosphere in the farm precincts, a delicious seasonal aroma.

PICKING UP APPLES

It was not apple picking but picking up apples! None were picked, they were shaken or knocked down from the trees with long poles. Bruising did not matter and the rotting ones were included too. There was no sorting out process. Large heaps were made about the orchard and then collected in apple barrels - wooden casks with rope loops at the sides for carrying. Some of the farm labourers' wives were often engaged for picking up apples and in one or two seasons I earned a shilling or two doing it for Farmer Jones.

Apples were put in the cider press without any special inspection, not even washed. The landlord of the Full Quart Inn had an orchard where several trees overhung a very black muddy ditch, consequently, a large number fell in it - they were rescued by using a sieve fastened to a pole and all went for cider!

My father always had a four and a half gallon cask at Christmas, generally given by Farmer Jones in recognition of his assistance at haymaking time.

WINTER EVENINGS

We spent our winter evenings in the warm little kitchen with the one oil lamp in the centre of the table and by today's standards it was very poor illumination. Sometimes we played our games of Ludo, Snakes and Ladders or Tiddly Winks but often mother and my sisters were engaged in needlework, while I spent my evenings doing fretwork - using wood from three-ply tea chests bought from the grocer's for a few coppers. A railway signalman, Mr Gurnet, who came from Yatton to work in the signal box on Sundays, brought me designs for making ornamental brackets. The designs were published by Hobbies Limited, who specialised in all forms of fretwork equipment. I made several attractive articles - one design in particular was for a pair of crescent moon shaped brackets of which my mother was very proud. She hung them in her sitting room at Hewish and later at Congresbury, but when she died and the home was broken up, they came back to me and now hang on the wall in my kitchen-diner.

About that time mother was in hospital for a few weeks and from one of my designs I cut out in ornamental lettering "HOME SWEET HOME" and backed it with some red material, like velvet, to greet mother on her homecoming. From an old wooden box I made a tool cupboard in which I kept all my fretwork tools, fretsaw, a tiny hammer, glasspaper, books and designs and other sundry treasures. I fitted a door and secured it with a small padlock costing threepence. Although I suppose it was not a thing of beauty, mother allowed me to keep it in a corner of the kitchen at Hewish Crossing, and it was my very proud possession!

My sisters who spent most evenings doing some form of needlework always grumbled at the grating noise of my fretsaw when I set up my fret-table clamped to the kitchen table. "Oh, not that noise again tonight?" So I had to compromise and do something quieter occasionally. I then started cleaning up and painting old horseshoes for ornaments. I coloured them with a cheap red enamel paint and then painted a motto around them in white lettering. One could often pick up a cast horseshoe on the road or around a farmyard, now a rarity. Those winter evenings make pleasant memories.

In our earlier years we had a little magic lantern and occasionally we persuaded father to put it on for us. It was a tiny oil lamp with a couple of adjustable lenses and with it about half a dozen slides with 5 or 6 pictures on each. We knew which picture was coming up next but our favourite one was where a man's dinner was flying away and he was holding up his knife and fork in horror!

Brother Harold also had a little vertical steam engine which was previously the toy of one of our Bridgwater cousins. He could only use it when he had a few coppers to buy some methylated spirit to put in the firebox.

We did not read much as we had so few books. What we possessed were our Sunday School prizes and a few books from our attendance at the chapel "Band of Hope" and "Christian Endeavour" meetings. Two of our favourites were "Christy's Old Organ" and "Froggy's little brother" and we had read them over and over.

Mother seemed to be always sewing or darning socks and Kathleen and Gertrude were generally doing needlework. It was very warm and cosy in the small kitchen heated by the coal burning range, on the top of which stood the large black iron kettle. This was kept filled and stood on the far corner away from the ring immediately over the fire, where it kept almost on the boil and was singing all evening. The tune rising and falling and almost dying away as the temperature of the water varied. It was a very contented and soothing kind of sound and one which we have lost with the coming of gas and the electric kettle which provides boiling water within a couple of minutes. The kettle would hold five or six pints of water and was used to fill a smaller kettle placed directly over the hotter ring to boil quickly when needed. That sound seemed almost more musical and expressive then the contented purring of the cat.

On Saturdays we had porridge for breakfaSt. Mother used to buy loose porridge oats in seven pound bags. I don't think the quick type was available but if it was it was more expensive. So mother had a large iron saucepan slowly cooking on the stove during all Friday evening. We could not have had much milk with it at breakfast as we only had one pennyworth daily, week in week out. I always remember this as we fetched it from the farm down the lane and took fourteen pence to pay for it once a fortnight. Milk was a 1½ pence (old money) per pint so our pennyworth consisted of two thirds of a pint and this served the lot of us for breakfast and at tea time.

How mother stretched that two thirds of a pint seemed nothing short of a miracle and even that at times was short measure. Especially when the farmer served us, as it was dipped out of the churn with a pint measure, and then a quantity tipped back until it was an estimated two thirds. This seemed to present quite a problem for the farmer as he first tipped a quantity back into the churn and then in case it was more then one pennyworth, he kept tipping back a little more and eventually our can contained something nearer half a pint, but his wife was more generous. We could rely on good measure when she served us. We used to fetch it from the farm during milking time and it has since occurred to me that if mother could have afforded larger quantities there would have been the risk of TB, as regulations controlling cleanliness and hygienic conditions in those days were non-existent.

There could not have been much wrong with our daily diet as we all grew up strong and healthy with good appetites, always eating what was put in front of us and now all well past our eightieth birthdays. Brother Harold even had his own teeth. That is, he never required dentures up to the time of his death. We rarely bought any sweets but mother ordered some with her groceries once a fortnight - generally the acid drop kind which she kept in a jar on the mantelpiece and gave out one each after breakfast to eat on our way to school. There were never enough to last until the next grocery delivery.

Father was not always with us in the evenings - he was either on duty or in bed when on nights, but when he was home he often read the news from the daily paper to mother. At that time the paper was called The Morning Leader but later through various amalgamations it was changed to the Daily News and Leader and finally several years later it became the News Chronicle until recently when it ceased publication. The coming of radio and television, especially commercial TV with its brilliant pictorial advertisements, caused the loss of advertising revenue to the national dailies and various weekly and monthly periodicals were forced to close or be swallowed up by amalgamation with its stronger brother.

BREAKFAST, DINNER &TEA

From Mondays to Fridays we invariably had a good fried breakfaSt. The bacon was all fat with no lean at all, the sort of white fat bacon no longer procurable. The fat was fried out of it leaving nice crisp rashers, and the liquid fat was enough to well soak a thick slice of fried bread for each and a large helping of fried potatoes. We all grew up hale and hearty under the diet. As I have previously mentioned, we had an occasional fried egg each morning in spring when eggs were very cheap and in the autumn there was fried apple or mushrooms with the bacon, and often on the way to school I remember chewing a succulent piece of bacon rind.

Being near the school we always came home to dinner - usually cooked potatoes with various green vegetables from the garden, peas and beans in season, cabbage or broccoli served with meat and rich brown gravy, but no sweets or puddings after, except when we had cold dinner. Then we had scrumptious spotted dick, with a layer of treacle. We had to eat what was put in front of us and clean up our plates. If anyone left something over it was put before the offender to eat at teatime and then it was readily devoured. Then we often quarrelled about who left some!

For tea we had one or two slices of bread and butter followed by bread and jam but we rarely had bread, butter and a layer of jam. We finished up with a slice of mother's home made fruit cake - but no supper!

WINTER - LESSONS IN HANDWRITING

During some winter evenings of 1907/8 my father being dissatisfied with our style of handwriting, decided to give us some lessons in the calligraphic art. He was a splendid writer himself, copperplate style. So he purchased pens and books and we had to sit around the table and copy the examples he set at the top of each page. The pens then in general use were steel nibs fixed in a holder, now almost obsolete through the introduction of the ball point. One had to be careful when dipping in the ink as if too much was taken up it did not survive the journey from inkpot to copybook but shed its load, falling on the table cloth or book and that was serious.

Our style had to consist of thin upward and thicker downward strokes and it was necessary to have the right style of pen nib for this. Nib patterns went in numbers and a favourite one for copperplate was also called the Waverley. How I loathed those lessons and although there seemed to be little difference in father's style and the examples of those in our school books no doubt the exercise of our home lessons under father's supervision helped us to perfect the style. It was stressed both at home and at school the importance of holding the pen correctly and our copybooks at school contained an illustration on the inside cover showing how to place one's fingers around the pen holder and with the pen holders always pointing towards the shoulder.

FATHER'S EDUCATION

Here I think a few details of my father's education should prove interesting. Owing to him being the eldest of three children and his mother a widow he had to leave the village school at Ide when only ten had a half years of age in 1885 and commence work. He enjoyed learning and was loathe to leave his books for play. When the schoolmaster "Billy Hale" was told the day before he left he remarked, "What a terrible pity my son, a terrible pity!" Father then went to live with his father's brother, uncle Jeremiah in a small farmstead in Bridford. He was a thatcher by trade and father was to learn thatching. Around the harvest season uncle Jeremiah and father went from farm to farm thatching hay and corn ricks. When working on farms in villages further from home they slept on the job. Then their breakfast beverage was cider. Uncle rode on a pony from farm to farm and father walked alongside.

At other times of the year they repaired the thatched roofs of cottages in the surrounding villages. During wet weather they were engaged in making spars and straw ropes, both skilled jobs. Spars were willow pegs about 18" long, made by splitting willows and twisting them at an angle. They were used to peg in the straw ropes around the thatch to keep the straw in place. The straw ropes were made on what is called a spit and turner, a long bar surrounded by a square frame with a hook at one corner. It was essential to have a good supply of both articles available and on hand at thatching time. It was a tough life for a lad of father's age and his aunt Mary Ann was inclined to be hard and lacked warmth. On one occasion father, at supper time, left his cheese rind on his plate and it was put out for his breakfast next morning!

During one winter he attended a night school promoted by the vicar of Bridford, and an exercise book of his is in our possession and reveals a fine example of penmanship. We also have an exercise book of his father's (my grandfather's) from when he attended a night school at Ide and at that time the scholars had to provide their own lighting. Two of them shared a candle, placing it on the desk between them. Here too a fine style of copperplate is evident.

Father's younger brother, Jeremiah, had to stay on at school for two or three years after him. He was by no means scholarly and his manner of leaving school was in far different circumstances. Being detained after lessons for some misdemeanour, he escaped out of a window when the master's attention was momentarily diverted. A chase around the school buildings ensued and uncle, as he turned round a corner, stopped short, put his foot out and tripped up the master! Thus ended his school career.

In later years, my father left his uncle and entered the railway service. Then eventually his brother, on the strength of father's satisfactory reputation, was also taken on at a country station, but his hasty temper got the better of him and one day he picked up a gun, possibly the station master s, and fired it through the office door! So ended his railway career. He later joined the Metropolitan police and remained in the service until his retirement. Although less studious than his brother his style of penmanship was also of a high standard.

SCHOOL LIBRARY AT HEWISH

A locked cupboard in the schoolroom contained a selection of books which were available to residents. They were all covered in thick brown paper and their titles written thereon and numbered. The demand seemed very rare and I believe they were all supplied by the SPCK (Society for the Promotion of Christian Knowledge). It was no doubt a church innovation and the issue controlled and recorded by the vicar's wife, Mrs Robinson. I cannot recall any issued but possibly it happened after school hours.

MEDICAL EXAMINATIONS AT SCHOOL

About the year 1910 the first medical examinations of school children took place. Notes were sent out to parents informing them of the date of the medical officer's visit and stating the time the parent could attend to be present and be told the result of their child's examination. I know my mother welcomed this opportunity to hear and get a free medical opinion of each child's health. It was a lady who examined us - the infant classroom was used for a surgery and each child was measured for height by a special rule fixed to the wall which was kept there permanently. Also a weighing scale was provided and weights recorded. Each child was stripped and a stethoscope was applied to the cheSt. I was pronounced a healthy and sturdy lad which no doubt pleased mother.

I remember that this innovation was not approved by some parents and one farmer (a school manager and churchwarden incidentally) kept his children from school on that date.

TEETH

About the year 1912 we were notified that a school dentist would be visiting the school and we also had a talk on dental care. For further encouragement we were offered toothbrushes which had to be ordered through the schoolmaster. They cost twopence each and I remember they were made of cane. Toothpowder of course, we were quite unacquainted with and we were told to use ordinary table salt as a cleaning agent.

PARASITES

In those days fleas abounded plentifully and the cleaner children, through sitting near others who were flea ridden, frequently became infected. I know it was a source of anxiety to my mother and about this time a nurse paid periodic visits to examine children's heads and if one was found to be infected with "nits" the poor victim was given a note for the parent. This too was a constant anxiety to my mother and my sisters were regularly tortured with a very fine toothed comb being pulled through their hair with mother scanning for "nits" and applying some very strong louse killing pomade.

MEASLES AND MUMPS

During our schooldays none of us suffered any severe illnesses but we shared with others in the outbreak of measles, when the school closed until it subsided. I was about six years old and had to stay in bed. I remember mother did not segregate us during the epidemic, her idea being to induce us all to get it together and get it over. It was not realised at that time that measles could produce after effects of a serious nature causing in some cases life time handicaps but none of us suffered in that way.

While we were convalescing and still home from school we wandered around the nearby fields and gathered huge bunches of cowslips which sister Kathleen made up into large cowslip balls. Now all the wild cowslips have disappeared. At that time nearly every field was ablaze with their beautiful yellow blooms but now one cannot find a single cowslip plant. I can remember what a lovely spring time that was.

A few years later there was another school closure, this time owing to an outbreak of mumps to which we all fell victim. This was more painful than measles and we just moped around feeling very sorry for ourselves. Although we used to hear about the more serious epidemics of diptheria and scarlet fever our village was never affected, neither did any children suffer from TB.

TOOTHACHE

On my tenth or eleventh birthday it was not a case of "happy returns" as I had a very painful toothache all day. So next day I begged my parents to take me to Dr Anderson to have it out. My father and I cycled to Banwell during surgery hours for him to extract it. He, not being a dentist, did not possess the necessary means to inject the gum to kill the pain. He selected the tool for the job and gripped the offending tooth saying, "Now don't wake my baby who is in bed asleep". Then he pulled and I let out a terrific yell, but my yell lasted longer than the pain, severe though it was, it was just momentary. That I think cost father a shilling and as far as I was concerned, it was very well spent!

ABOUT MY SCHOOLMASTERS

MR PAGE

We all (except Ena our youngest sister) commenced our schooling under Mr Page. With a thick mass of snow white hair, rich side whiskers and a beard to match, he gave us the impression of being a very old man. He was what one would term "one of the old school", very strict and a very frequent wielder of the cane. To us he rarely displayed any form of good humour. We were very much afraid of him but by the standards of the day I think he could be regarded as a good schoolmaster but we learned very little beyond that what was termed the "three R s!" That was at a time when it was considered sufficient for children of ordinary working folk.

He was a staunch churchman and his daughter Frances (the cripple) was the organist until he retired and went to live in Weston in 1910. I remember that on Friday afternoons he spent the time at his desk printing in very elaborate style the numbers of the hymns to be sung on Sunday. It was in what I believe was called "Old English" and one copy was displayed in the church porch and the other in the church. He had two sons and two other daughters, one of whom died before we commenced school - her gravestone can be seen in the church yard. In spite of our fear of him I know we all felt sorry when he said goodbye to us on his last day at school.

MR J S GOWAR

Mr Page was succeeded by Mr J S Gowar and in our school routine it was the dawn of a new era! Firstly the slates were discarded and new history and geography books were introduced. Then followed dictionaries and our beloved system of going up and down in class, as previously mentioned, was no longer observed. He was a very keen musician and with a very sensitive ear our coarse country voices caused him to wince and take on a look of pain. Very gentlemanly in manner and appearance - he came to us at the age of 28 and impressed us and everyone else by attending church on Sundays in a black silk top hat! But after a while he resorted to a bowler, probably becoming aware that the top hat appeared somewhat out of place in a strictly rural community.

He was what is termed a "dapper sort of chap", being of slight build and very smart in his movements. He had a smartly waxed moustache ending with long pointed waxed spurs at each side and which he was fond of twirling with his fingers during lessons. His arrival coincided with the coming of the Revd Blathwayt and with them it was arranged that on Wednesday mornings instead of our scripture lesson we marched into church for a children's service for which Mr Gowar was organiSt. On going back into school, if he was displeased with our hymn singing he "let us have it good and proper" and we had to go through the hymns over again, interspersed with harsh criticisms.

Mr Gowar was essentially a city man and good manners were a strong point with him. In school it was on the toes as we walked about the school room and we had to knock at the door before entering a classroom, a form of behaviour unknown to us previously. He was not interested in sport and he only appeared in the playground on fine mornings for strict drilling lessons, but at Christmas for our last lesson on breaking up day he organised a concert. He taught a few boys and girls with better voices to sing suitable songs and others to recite. His wife was also a teacher and she always taught the lower standards.

She was inclined to be severe but we were all very sorry when they left to take another post at Nailsea.

MR F P FARR

Mr Gowar was succeeded by Mr Farr who came to us from Mark, and again we sensed a change in the scholastic atmosphere. Mr Farr's manner was more relaxed, at playtime as we could not play football or cricket through lack of equipment, he joined us in games of rounders. He soon began to call the boys by their nicknames both during lessons and in the playground. Occasionally he arrived in school displaying a short temper and his bad mood lasted nearly all day.

He was intensely patriotic and on Empire Day we all assembled in the playground to salute the flag and sing Empire songs - such as "Flag of Britain proudly waving over many distant seas" and "God of our Fathers Known of Old" and it was not surprising that in 1914 when the war was declared in August of that year Mr Farr volunteered for war service and eventually served in Salonica.

As I have mentioned elsewhere, he organised our Scout Troop. After the war he was appointed to the Headship of Congresbury school. I was indebted to him for an excellent reference which it was necessary for me to produce with my application to enter the railway service.

Mr Farr was succeeded by Mr Bell but he was my schoolmaster only for a few months.

Hewish School Photo about 1908 - Mr Page on right.
Arthur Westcott - bottom row - last on right
Gertrude Westcott - 2nd row up - 2nd from right
Kathleen Westcott - 3rd row up - 4th from right
Harold Westcott - 5th row up - 4th from right

ANNUAL SCRIPTURE EXAMS

Once a year, usually around Easter time, an inspector came to test us on our knowledge of Scripture. During the year we followed a syllabus which laid down a study of certain Old Testament stories and a section of New Testament teachings. We were questioned on them and also on our knowledge of the Church of England Catechism. The inspector was always a Church of England clergyman and the examination took the whole of the morning. Then we were given the afternoon as a half-day's holiday.

MY BROTHER HAROLD

Brother Harold was three and a half years my senior and on that account I regarded him as a superior being, conversely he regarded me as being inferior and when boys of his own age were about to play with him, I was very much "de-trop" and he would not tolerate my company. On one occasion when with a few of his companions he wandered off across the fields I followed at a respectful distance, ignoring his shouts of "go back". He then ran back and gave me a terrific punch in the stomach. I did not cry but I went very pale and then Harold was frightened and he went pale too! With visions of trouble if I went back home in that state he placated me by allowing me to join them!

If at home on occasions when mother found fault or was cross with him, Harold would adopt a very grumpy tone "I'll run away, I will! I'll run away!" How mother used to laugh back with a remark "You won t run very far my son, you will soon come back!" On one particular occasion mother criticised him over the polishing of my sisters Sunday boots and told him to do them again and use more elbow grease. Out came the usual grumpy remark - "I'll run away I will!" I overheard him and it fired my imagination. As soon as mother was out of hearing I said to him "Come on, let's do it!" I was so enthusiastic that he agreed and said "We ll do it as soon as we get home from school this afternoon." "Good!" So on arrival from school I promptly reminded Harold "Now we've got to run away". "Oh! ah! yes!" says Harold. "Let's go". So we went out into our lane and ran very fast down to the first field gate. Then I stopped, "Here!" I said, "it's no good going this way, this only leads to the fields". "We must go the other way". "Oh-ah! Yes" says Harold. Then, "Here, we can't very well go tonight we've got to go to Christian Endeavour meeting this evening". We went back indoors and so ended our daring escape.

We often quarrelled and bickered but this was the generally accepted behaviour in families with brothers of disparate ages and in later years Harold was the best brother a brother ever had! Often when discussing problems of a domestic nature or matters connected with our employment (we were both station masters) he sought my opinion and indeed he sometimes treated me as if I were the elder and more mature then he! I have already related how he saved me from drowning on two occasions.

In my earlier years at school I remember Harold with the bigger boys often played the game of ducky. I never played it and it was never played by the boys of my age. Each player had their own ducky stones and they were often on the look out to find a good "ducky stone". A term used in the game was "pankying up" and this was the means of deciding who should be the first player to go "ducky". They each threw their stone against a large boulder and the one whose stone landed further from it was the one to go "ducky". He then placed his ducky stone on top of the larger one for the others to throw theirs and knock if off. I forget what happened next and even Harold in later years when reminiscing over our school days often referred to it but could not recall the final rules although he would often remark when out and about "that would make a good ducky stone for pankying up". It has occurred to me that it was related to a game some grown-ups played called Pitch and Toss but instead of using stones they played with coppers a gambling game of course.

PUXTON CHILDREN

The children from Puxton all came to our school. There were several families and for some unknown reason we tended to regard them as a "race apart". It may have been because none of them were very scholarly and for this reason it may well have been our headmaster who seemed to hold them in similar regard. It was a long walk for them around the road but a fairly short distance when they came across the fields, which they did except in very wet weather. On an occasion when they were told to write a composition about their village, one lad concluded his effort with the sentence, "Puxton is a knowledgeable place!" This raised a laugh when the headmaster read it out to the class and ever after in the playground we often quoted it in mockery to any Puxton scholar.

There was a very old school at Puxton, consisting of one room and a small enclosure as a play yard. It was situated at the end of the village green but must have been closed in the last century. It remained intact with a number of school forms and was used for parish and election meetings until about 1970 when it was vandalised and eventually demolished. It was probably a "Dame School" and if there are any records about, its history should prove interesting.

GENERAL ELECTION FIGHTS

During General Election times feelings ran very high among the grown ups, and when a political meeting was held in the school they became rowdy and often resulted in a fight or two outside at the close of the meeting. The farming fraternity were all Conservative, their labourers, mainly through ignorance felt obliged to vote the same as their masters and it is pretty certain that neither masters nor men could sustain an intelligent argument on the main questions before the electorate.

Liberals were in a minority. My father and Mr Bailey (his colleague) were the main proponents of Liberalism in the village and they were able to influence a few labourers to favour their cause but they were the only ones who saw a daily newspaper, as I have mentioned earlier. Now the rivalry of the two parties spread to the children and we who proudly wore a red rosette came up against the blues and heated arguments developed sometimes resulting in coming to blows.

My father and Mr Bailey obtained huge election posters to exhibit, but as we were living down the lane where posters would not be seen father had permission to erect them in Mr Ball's orchard at the top of the lane on the main road. During the night they were covered by thick black mud sloshed over them by the bucket full, but they were patiently washed down or renewed. I remember one huge poster in particular - it portrayed the *"Honest, British workman"* with his tool bag slung over his shoulder, wearing corduroy trousers with straps around them just below the knee (generally called "Yorks" locally - and always worn by navvies). He is approached by a bowler hatted city gent saying, *"Think my good man if you vote Liberal your beer and tobacco will be taxed more heavily"* and the noble reply was *"Better my baccy than my children's bread!"*

Although that was in 1906 and I was only 6 years of age, I was greatly impressed by that poster and in my infantile mind I thought that was an irrefutable argument for voting Liberal!

THE HUMMING BIRD

Mr A E Collard was the landlord of the Full Quart Inn and by us boys he was always referred to as the "Hummingbird", on account of his frequent and very loud humming. For no particular reason he was not very popular with us and I think that was an attitude we caught from the grown ups, as I cannot recall that we had any cause to nurse feelings of hostility against him. On one occasion though, when the plums were ripe, and Mr Collard had a tree heavily laden overhanging the road in the lane leading down to the railway crossing, the time seemed ripe for us to knock a few off by stone throwing. We crept along very low under the hedge and were preparing to have a throw when we heard the loud familiar humming and then we espied Mr Collard up among the branches filling a basket. That was a lucky escape as I know he would have informed our parents and there would have been trouble!

Mr Collard used to walk the fields near the crossing to keep a daily check on the livestock belonging to Farmer Gill who lived about four miles distant at Rolstone. Now in those fields around blackberry time there were several mushroom "rings" and Mr Collard who was about early in the morning, had the first picking. If any in the ring were only just showing through in form of buttons, he carefully covered them with a layer of grass. We were aware of this little trick, it was to hide them from view as they grew during the day and often by the time we came along in the evening some of them were large enough for us to pick. Then in return for Mr Collard's consideration we made a point of picking some grass and covering any wet juicy cowpats which happened to be in the ring in the hope that Mr Collard would draw his hand through it mistaking it for a mushroom! I doubt if the trick ever worked but we were satisfied that one good turn deserved another!

Mr Collard really achieved fame by the collapse of his newly erected hayrick. It happened about 1912. Mr Collard had a small paddock adjoining the pub in which he salvaged the hay to feed his pony throughout the winter. On this particular occasion he enlisted the aid of my father for a few hours in the morning to build a rick in the corner of the paddock. Then later in the day a few more volunteers turned up and the story is best related in a poem composed by Mr

Bailey and which appeared in the two Weston weekly newspapers, The Mercury and The Gazette. Jim Bailey reported regularly to both papers any news and incidents relating to Hewish. There was a regular column appearing each week headed, "Have you heard that?",, Under which appeared any amusing occurrences of a personal nature. It was a very popular column read by all the locals and Mr Bailey's poetic contribution was the talk of the parish. It should be remembered that as no one took any London dailies, national and political news were rarely prominent in people's minds, so the amusing poem relating to Mr Collard's hayrick proved a real gem to all and sundry!

The main characters involved were:

My lad from Devon - my father, John Westcott.
My Lord - Mr Millard, Landlord of the White Hart Inn as Mr Collard facetiously addressed him as in the poem.
The man on the red bike was Basil Light the postman
The Full Tankard was the Full Quart Inn as the sign outside was an illustration of a foaming tankard of beer.
It was appropriately headed with a couplet viz, "Huntman's Double" may win the Royal Hunt Cup, "But Landlord's double can't put a little rick up!"

It ran thus:

Twas on a glorious day in June,
    when the Humming bird was in full tune.
The hay was dry and fit to be carried
    as from the Full Tankard the landlord sallied.
Political foes he approached without fear;
    it may be he promised them plenty of beer!
He confessed a hayrick he never had made
    and to do so now he felt quite afraid.
So shortly after the hour of seven,
    he collar(e)d the help of My lad from Devon.
This kind friend he mounted the staddle,
    Amid cartloads of "thank yous" and that sort of twaddle.
And just as the work was about to begin,
    no less a person than MiLord dropped in.
With his White H(e)art full of brotherly love
    big pitches of hay he aloft did shove.
While to keep their minds and intellect clear,
    they diluted the cider with ginger beer.
The rick was well started and began to get higher.

When the "maker" found himself bound to retire.
Whereupon "MiLord" like a real live peer
        defied the consequences seeing no fear.
He'd made ricks before, he exclaimed quite loud
        and to do so again he would feel quite proud.
Then a cyclist passing on a red bike quoth he
        "Pitching hay is just what I like".
And all went well as a marriage bell,
        but a sadden part I've yet to tell!
The cyclist paused on his work of love,
        just to case his well trained eye above.
And in so doing issued a warning to his Lordship above,
        who the idea scoring,
Replied in a huff, "The rick's right enough,
        get on with your nonsense and shove up the stuff!"
"Look out!" What the
        .... Alas!
It's the talk of the town how that rick fell down
        Amid language of purple, blue and brown!
But the sight of foaming Full Quarts of beer
        set some farmhands at work with jolly good cheer.
And the rick was re-made in the cool evening shade
        but landlords have yet to learn how hayricks are made.

                          J Bailey.

NOTE: The White Hart Inn was renamed "The Palmer's Elm Inn" and in 2003
became a Chinese Restaurant.

One of father's favourite "Budget" jokes!

Father on duty in the signal box often exchanged pleasantries with
neighbours passing over the crossing and on one occasion -

"Well Oliver I wonder what the Budget will hold for us when it
comes out next week?"

"Oh!" says Oliver, "Is that next week? I shall have to get one o'
they if it costs me a weeks wages!"

DAILY NEWSPAPERS

The day to day excitement of the war and the eager thirst for news induced a newsagent from Worle to extend his daily round to Hewish. Also Mr Farr our schoolmaster, persuaded a boy, Ernest Neath, who left school in the summer of 1914, to start a paper round so we were all kept well up to date with war news.

I was very active with the Scouts, making the most of the last days, knowing I should be leaving home as soon as a vacancy on the railway occurred.

HOUSE REMOVAL

Around this time my father was promoted to a post at Puxton station signal box and as the Crossing House at Hewish was provided for a signalman there, my father was under an obligation to vacate it. The Crossing House at that time was one of the best and most recent dwelling houses in the district, although it was originally built in the 19th century to accommodate a resident crossing keeper to control the level crossing gates. There being no suitable cottage available my father, early in 1914, negotiated with the owner of a field, where a triangular piece about ¼ acre ran alongside the main road about ¾ mile further down on the Weston side of the village and on the right hand side a few hundred yards past the White Hart Inn (recently and more appropriately named The Palmer's Elm Inn as that little area was known by that name and nearby was the Palmer's Elm Chapel).

The cost of the land was £40 (forty pounds) and was paid for in ready cash which I think constituted the bulk of father's savings. He then arranged a mortgage to erect the house, with the Co-operative Wholesale Society for £195.00. After drawing out his own plans he had to get them approved by the Axbridge District Council.

At that period no doubt planning regulations were much more relaxed than today (no drainage or sewerage problems). The main requirement being a settling tank for waste water from the house, which consisted of two bricklined pits, a small one filled with clinkers to serve as a filter before the water passed into the larger settling tank.

The lavatory was an earth closet, common to most cottages, which consisted of a large bucket and the contents were buried in the garden. In some cases cottages had a cess-pit which had to be emptied by hand dipping about once a year and the contents scattered over the garden.

Bathrooms were non existent as obviously without mains water they were not a practical proposition. The weekly bath had to be filled by hand dipping from the copper boiler, this being a standard item for every cottage. I do not think my father's plans would pass today, thorough and painstaking though they were. They of course lacked the professional efforts of an architect. Very few houses were being built in the villages and ours in 1914 was the first new cottage to be built in Hewish this century. A builder, who came into the village at about the same time, erected a pair of semi-detached cottages which could not be sold and for several years the builder and his family occupied both.

At the same time he erected a large galvanised iron garage opposite to run a car hire service and sold petrol in one gallon tins (petrol pumps were then unknown). His petrol sales were to passing motorists who now were beginning to be more frequent but still very few passed through daily.

OUR NEW HOME - HOMELEA

While the builder's houses were situated at the extreme end of Hewish on the Bristol side, our cottage was almost the last at the Weston end. To consider father's plans for authority to build, a representative from Axbridge District Council came over by horse and trap and no problems arose so my father was given permission to build. To save expense he dug out the footings himself and our baby sister, Ena aged 8, dug the first turf on the site of the front door as we stood around to witness and drink to the success of the operation in cold tea! The house was completed just at the time of the outbreak of the 1914-18 war and we moved down in September. It was during that Autumn that grandma Westcott died at Exeter and it was on the occasion of my visit to assist my Aunt Emily to clear up her rooms when I acquired the wonderful pocket knife previously mentioned.

Our house contained three bedrooms and the two larger ones had a firegrate and downstairs in the scullery was the built-in copper boiler across one corner, but a few years later portable iron boilers were installed in the newer houses and then when electrical power became widespread even those were superceded by the twin-tub washing machine. In place of the all important water barrel we had a large circular galvanised iron cistern with a tap because this had to be our drinking water supply as we were about a quarter of a mile from the river. It was erected on a brick built stand just outside the back door.

The outdoor privy was also situated near-by and was a wooden hut furnished with a bucket. With no continuous water supply all country houses lacked any form of indoor sanitation. The bedrooms were furnished with wooden and marble topped wash stands to carry a large china water jug with a wash basin and even more importantly two chamber pots, usually kept under the bed - one on each side! (His and her's). Sometimes they were retained in small wooden cabinets. In less refined times they were often referred to as "what goes under" and euphemistically the "gazunder".

Homelea -Hewish - Built 1914 for John Westcott
Twins Arthur & Gertie   (photo in 1920's)

LAST DAYS AT SCHOOL

I celebrated my fourteenth birthday on 7 September 1914 and that was school leaving age, but as I was on the waiting list to commence as a lad porter on the railway (it was the Great Western railway then) I stayed on at school until the Spring of 1915. Soon after Christmas I was vaccinated by our local Dr Anderson, as this was a requirement of the railway company. The company also required three testimonials as to character and I obtained one from the schoolmaster and one from our vicar, the Revd Blathwayt, and I forget who provided my third. Those last few months seemed very exciting and eventful. Mr Farr our schoolmaster enlisted for war service and finished teaching when we broke up for our Easter holidays. I made the most of my remaining scouting days and at Christmas I had my photograph taken in my full scouts rig-out in a studio at Weston. My corporal, Ted, also had his taken at the same time.

THE "LABOUR EXAM"

During my schooldays a system existed whereby a scholar of about 12 years of age was allowed to leave school provided he reached a certain standard. This proved a great advantage to labouring families as it enabled a successful lad to go to work on a farm and so augment the family income by two or three shillings weekly.

PRIZEGIVING

During February 1915 the school prizegiving took place. This was a recent annual innovation, unknown to us in earlier years. The awards were mainly for good attendance but on this occasion I was not present on account of my vaccination arm. It was therefore a great surprise to be told that I was awarded a prize for popularity by the vote of the school children. It was one of G D Robert's books, "More Kindred of the Wild" containing interesting tales of various wild animals. I was then a half timer on account of my being past school leaving age but was allowed to be absent on half days. I was very proud of this award.

It was of course the early months of the First World War and the local and national news was centred around the accounts of the Western Front and the local papers reported about men from the Weston area who were on active service. News was now coming back of those wounded or killed in action.

Arthur Westcott - Patrol Leader in Scouts - 1914

GARDENING 1915

During the spring of 1915, being as I have already mentioned a half timer at school, it was decided that I could work in the garden of Mr John Ball who was our nearest neighbour at Hewish Crossing and lived on the corner at the top of the lane opposite the Full Quart Inn. He was a railway pensioner and a widower and had now reached the age when he could no longer cultivate the garden himself. His was a very large garden and he also had an orchard adjoining which extended down to the railway line at the crossing. He also had another orchard on the opposite side of the main road (A370) where in one corner were the ruins of a derelict cottage.

Mr Ball also kept a pony, Victor, and a cart. After I had done a day's digging and planting, I had to groom the pony, brushing him down and curry combing after which I exercised him by riding bare back up and down the road - most enjoyable. I worked until April when on the 26th I went off to Wookey to start my railway career. For the season's work Mr Ball gave me 12s 6d (62½ new pence) and this went a long way towards paying for my first set of long trousers. In our day no boy wore long trousers until he left school.

GROWING UP

Now in the spring of 1915 the subject of our careers was the predominant topic of conversation in the family. We began to realise that all four of us, Harold, Kathleen, Gertude and I were about to commence a new chapter in the course of our lives and the joys of schooldays were about to be replaced by the problems of setting out to earn our own livings.

I remember when Harold left home in 1911 to work at Wookey station mother threw an old shoe after him for luck!

Kathleen was now a pupil teacher at the school and she was the first ever to launch out into the teaching profession from our school. She finished as a scholar on reaching the age of fourteen years and the following week she was appointed as a Pupil Teacher Candidate Monitress and I remember the headmaster Mr Farr, announcing to the whole school that Kathleen Westcott had left school and from now on she is a teacher and must be addressed as Miss Westcott. This was sensational and it did not go down well with some mothers in the village. There were sarcastic undertones when they passed us on the road in which the words, Miss Westcott, could be plainly heard. Several years later Kathleen became headmistress of the school.

My twin sister Gertrude was never very happy at school and made little headway with most lessons although she was a very neat writer and fond of painting and drawing. I was always well ahead of her but until we reached standard three our schoolmaster kept me back when I should have gone forward with other boys and girls to standards four and five merely because I was a twin. But when his successor Mr Gowar came he was astonished that for such a reason I was kept back and I was immediately moved up a standard to join with and hold my own with the other boys and girls of my age.

So on Gertrude's 14th birthday she was ready to go to school as usual, when father told her she need not go anymore and she could not have had a more acceptable birthday present! As I have already mentioned, I stayed on as a half timer until I was sent for to commence my railway service in the following April. Gertrude was eventually apprenticed to the dressmaking trade with a lady in Weston and cycled to and fro daily along with several of her schoolgirl friends most of whom obtained jobs as shop assistants. It was often a very hard and icy cold ride during the winter months but there was no other means of making the journey as a bus service had not yet commenced.

Sister Ena, being the baby of the family, had to continue at school for another six years, until reaching the age of 14 in 1920. She then became a Pupil Teacher Candidate Monitoress and eventually entered the teaching profession and continued until her subsequent marriage.

SOME THINGS WE HAVE LOST!

With the advance of modern methods in matters domestic and in farming activities there are sounds which were pleasant and soothing to the ear which are now lost to us. I have already mentioned the kettle on the hob being kept just off the boil all the evening.

There was very early on a fine summer morning, the sound of a horse drawn mowing machine.

Then the crowing of the roosters on a moonlit night. I remember it seemed as if ours started crowing loudly down in the fowl house, to be answered by another crowing down at the farm. This was followed by another answering at a more distant farm and then another, and then another further and further away until it seemed to me that the whole country was linked up with cocks crowing. This has gone with the introduction of day old chicks supplied commercially and the disappearance of barnyard poultry keeping.

FINIS

My dear grand daughters,

Now here are the memories of my schooldays as promised you a few years ago and I hope you will find them interesting although they lack any form of sensationalism, neither are they in chronological order and the desultory manner in which they are written arises from the fact that as some struck a chord in my memory, I penned them forthwith. It is as if I put all the incidents in a sack, then turned them out in a heap and picked out one at random!

But in recalling them, I seem to have lived over again those halcyon days leaving a warm nostalgic afterglow!

Sadly, all the schoolmates involved in these memories are now no more and in the words of the Prophet Elijah;

"I, even I only am left".

Your affectionate grandpa
Arthur James Westcott.

(Family nickname from infancy, "Pog") but at school nicknamed "Muggins" and afterwards the two were merged to become "Poggins" by which I am now called by nephews and nieces of all ages!

I recall memories of:

"Bufty" Neath - Ernest, ginger hair	"Tacker" Beacham- Oliver
"Bottle" Williams - Frank	"Baker" Wreford - Ted
"Brownie" - Lewis Edwards	"Lorrie" Kimmins - Arthur
"Jacket" - Brother Harold	"Peckham" - Bill Cox
"Sparrow Cox" - Harry	"Nicky" - Bill Nicholls
"Wormy" - Ted Nicholls	"Joner" - Harold Jones
"Durby" Davis - Walter	"Poodle Davis" - sister

and many others who never boasted a nickname!

I have had playmates, I have had companions,
In my days of childhood, in my joyful schooldays
All, all are gone, the old familiar faces
How some they have died and some they have left me
And some are taken from me; all are departed
All, all are gone, the old familiar faces.

C.Lamb

Little Angels: Nazareth House Children's Home in Cape Town

What Does it Take To Take in a Child?

Imagine sitting by a cot holding a baby's hand and watching her die.

Imagine choosing to do so.

When Pat and Phillip van Rensburg set up Little Angels, an emergency care home for abandoned babies in Cape Town, they knew they would face losing some. Five years and 106 babies later, only nine have died from AIDS-related illnesses.

Four of the babies currently in their care have tested HIV positive. But the van Rensburgs have a long wait before they will know the infants' final status. Babies born to HIV positive women can carry their mother's antibodies and can't therefore test positive until they are eighteen months old. Pat and Phillip rely on hope, prayer and TLC to deal with the uncertainty.

"It's all about love and good nutrition," says Pat. *"When you hear where some have come from, you realise they wouldn't have stood a chance. Proper care, good food and as much love and physical contact as we can give makes all the difference."* Take, for example, the baby found covered with maggots in a drain, or the newborn abandoned in a plastic bag on a train line. Both are now picking up weight at Little Angels.

The love and physical contact come in unlimited supply from Pat, Phillip and the four house mothers of Little Angels. Nearly all the other baby baggage food, nappies, clothes, cots and toys has been donated.

"We've had no government help, just private gifts," says Phillip. *"God has blessed us so much. Most of our medical help is free. And we rely on friends to donate nappies."*

With an ever-changing number of babies in their care - from day to day they don't know who might arrive and who will find another home - that's quite a nappy tower. The van Rensburgs have applied to adopt two of the youngsters; the other two are waiting to be placed with families. The couple's dream is to care for up to twenty children at a time, providing a temporary home until they can be placed, either back in their communities or with adoptive parents.

Although community placement is the legal preference, finding a family of the same race or culture for a child isn't always easy. However, the van Rensburgs live in hope.

"That's why we chose not to be a long term facility," says Pat. *"We want to be a family home while the children need one, but not take them out of their culture."* About 15% of the babies have been placed back in their communities. But with a government grant of only R100-400 per month for fostering, and no financial help for adoption, many families cannot afford to take in another child. Other options are local mixed-race fostering or adoption. But most of the van Rensburgs' tiny charges have, so far, gone overseas for adoption.

A recent study commissioned by the South African government found that AIDS was the biggest cause of maternal death is South Africa between 1999 and 2001. Estimated at 17%, the true percentage is now thought to be much higher. Whatever the actual figure, the need to take in orphans and abandoned children is rocketing, vouches Jane Payne, the social worker at Nazareth House Children's Home in Cape Town.

"The way forward in South Africa has to be fostering in some form we need people out there who are prepared to take a child in but the whole process has to be done properly, with proper screening and monitoring by social workers and good care for the children."

'Doing it properly' has meant a huge new home for the van Rensburgs. When Phillip was retrenched two years ago, after twenty years in a bank, they bought a dilapidated mansion in a smart Cape Town suburb.

"We wanted to be somewhere with rich neighbours who could fork out for the children," he laughs. But it didn't go quite according to plan. Abusive phone calls decrying *"blacks moving into the area"* and negative reporting in the local press greeted the van Rensburgs. *"One neighbour banged on our gate and threatened to burn the house down."*

Even without such opposition, the challenges of taking in abandoned, often sick, babies would be too much for many well-intentioned couples. First the physical demands: washing and feeding the children; visiting doctors and hospitals, and keeping the house extra clean in the presence of the HI virus. And then the emotional drains: pacifying crying babies; dealing with toddler tantrums, and growing to love dying children.

"*With an HIV positive child, when they're really sick you've got to be there,*" says Jane Payne. "*Night times you'll be woken up, daytimes you'll be back and forth to the hospital. You can't just get rid of the child when times get tough.*" She advises would-be carers to analyse their motives carefully. "*The best reasons to take in children? They probably include wanting to give them a loving home while realising they can't meet all your needs. A lot of people see a little child who's sick and just want to love and care for him or her. But it doesn't end there. Soothing temper tantrums or cleaning up vomit that's what loving a child really is.*"

The van Rensburgs' motivation is enviably simple.

"*It's our calling from God,*" says Pat. "*We love children and want to provide a caring home with warmth, laughter and hugs. If a baby is dying, let him at least know love and affection in his short time on earth.*" Which is not to say a death doesn't hurt deeply. "*Of course it's traumatic but we have had counselling and learned mechanisms to 'help' with the mourning, like talking about the child a lot, and keeping photos.*" And underlying the grief must be the comfort of knowing they have lavished love on a child who may otherwise have known none.

The simplest of callings, the greatest of challenges. Who is up to the task the van Rensburgs have taken on as the number of orphaned and abandoned babies grows in South Africa?

"*Taking in kids is the only way forward, though it has to be supervised wherever possible,*" says Jane Payne. "*It won't be the perfect situation but we've just got to do the best we can.*"

Debbie Thomas